An American Muslim Preacher

Nuances of Islam in the West

Sayed Moustafa Al-Qazwini, PhD

Islamic Educational Center of Orange County

An American Muslim Preacher: Nuances of Islam in the West

Sayed Moustafa Al-Qazwini, PhD

First Published in 2017 by
Islamic Educational Center of Orange County
3194-B Airport Loop Drive
Costa Mesa, California 92626
Tel: (714) 432-0060

Website: **www.iecoc.org**
E-mail: **info@iecoc.org**

YouTube IECOC
@IECOC
@IECOC

ISBN 978-0-9989055-0-1

Cover Design and Layout by Islamic Publishing House (www.iph.ca)

Contents

Introduction

In the Name of God, the Most Gracious, the Most Merciful. All praise is due to God, Lord of the universe, and may the peace and blessings of God be upon all of His prophets and messengers, including His final messenger Muḥammad, and his pure and immaculate household and righteous companions.

Throughout my numerous years of Islamic preaching and educational work in the West, and in particular in the United States of America, I have noticed an astounding rise in both the level of quality and quantity of Islamic preaching. These developments have been due to an increase in both amount of the resources utilized and the number of educators in America. As for its resources, the American Muslim communities have been able to adapt to its contemporary needs by utilizing appropriate means such as social media, the establishment of educational and community organizations, and engagement in the civic and interfaith aspects of life in America. The number and quality of Islamic educators has also increased, with greater attention being paid to the social and moral needs of the communities, as well as a rise in the number of younger educators who are more attuned to the various needs of the people. Thus, I can say with confidence that the current state of Islamic preaching in the United States of America looks fairly positive. However, it is important to ask whether the present and future state of Islamic preaching in this country can be sustained or not. In other words, will the American Muslim community be successful in undertaking this significant task in a positive and effective manner, especially taking into consideration the recent and numerous challenges that they continue to face? It is this question that forms the basis of this work. My contention is that successful Islamic preaching will continue to pose a formidable challenge for the American Muslim community, but will certainly be promising if a number of crucial points are adhered to, some of which will be elaborated during the course of this work.

While the title of this work is *An American Muslim Preacher: Nuances of Islam in the West*, I will employ the Arabic terms *daʿwah* and *tablīgh* throughout the book to refer to what may loosely be considered Islamic preaching. This is because there are no accurate English translations to the concepts of daʿwah and tablīgh. Thus, within the context and scope of this book, I will employ the term daʿwah to refer specifically to the process of educating and inviting non-Muslims to knowledge and awareness of Islam in the West. On the other hand, I will employ the term tablīgh to specify the process of preaching to and teaching the Western Muslim community.

The results of this work are based mainly on over three decades of personal research and observations, supplemented with interviews conducted with various activists, scholars, educators, and academics in the United States. These include both men and women, and Sunnī and Shīʿa, who are committed to daʿwah and tablīgh initiatives in various forms across America.

Discussions in this work will proceed in the following manner: In the first chapter, I will discuss the concepts of daʿwah and tablīgh, including their linguistic and technical meanings, their significance, their objectives, and their underpinnings. I will further contrast these meanings and their significance with other religious traditions. In the second chapter, I will present an overview of my area of case study, that is, the United States of America. I will discuss the religious, social, and political identities of the American landscape. In chapter three, I will elaborate on the history and rise of Islam and Muslims in the United States, and the state of Islam and Muslims in contemporary America. Chapter four will include my discussion on daʿwah and tablīgh specifically in the context of the West. This will include a presentation of the objectives, approaches, capabilities, and impediments of daʿwah and tablīgh in America, as well as the characteristics of a preacher in this context. Furthermore, I will discuss important topics such as interfaith and intra-faith dialogue. Finally, I will close with a summary of my arguments and some closing recommendations.

This work is based on my PhD dissertation, completed at the International Colleges of Islamic Sciences in London. I would like to acknowledge and thank my respected academic advisor - the honorable Ayatullah Dr. Sayed Fadhil al-Milani for his continued guidance and sagacious insights during the course of the composition of my doctoral dissertation. I would also like to thank Dr. Ibrahim al-Ati, Dr. Sayed Kadom Shubber, Dr. Oliver Scharbrodt, and Dr. Sayed Ihsan al-Shahristani for their crucial recommendations and advice, as well as the rest of the faculty members at the International Colleges of Islamic Sciences. Additionally, I would like to thank my friends and colleagues across North America who were gracious enough to share their insights and experiences with me. I am indebted to Shaykh Saleem Bhimji and Sister Arifa Hudda for their efforts in editing, designing, and publishing this work. May God reward and grant them all success and honor in this life and in the Hereafter.

Finally, a note on translations and usage. All translations of Arabic texts, including the Qur'an, are my own - unless otherwise noted. It is customary that when the names of God, Prophet Muḥammad, other Prophets, or Imams are enunciated, they are followed by the following phrases: God – "Glorified and Exalted is He"; Prophet Muḥammad - "Peace be upon him and his family"; Prophets, Imams from the family of Prophet Muḥammad, and his daughter Fāṭima al-Zahrā' - "Peace be upon him/her." With great respect, admiration, recognition, and praise, I have omitted the mentioned phrases for the sake of continuity.

I pray that this humble work is accepted by my Lord, and is of benefit to the readers.

Dr. Sayed Moustafa al-Qazwini
December 2016/Rabīʿ al-Awwal 1438
Costa Mesa, California

Chapter One: Daʿwah and Tablīgh

The Linguistic and Conventional Meanings of Daʿwah and Tablīgh

The word daʿwah stems from the root *daʿā, yadʿū, duʿāʾan.* According to Ibn Manẓūr al-Afrīqī, daʿwah is the singular form of *duʿāʾ*, which is to call; and its plural form is *duʿāt* which is a group that calls for truth or falsehood.[1] According to Fairūzābādī, the noun is daʿwah and the verb is *yadʿū*, to invite.[2] Al-Jawharī states that daʿwah refers to a single call or to summon.[3] Al-Rāghib al-Isfahānī states that *al-duʿāʾ ilā ʿl-shayʾ* means to persuade adoption of something.[4] Thus, the linguistic meaning of daʿwah is to call, invite, or summon someone to something.

There are several conventional usages of the term daʿwah, which stem from the broadness of its connotation and the versatility of its denotation. Additionally, various usages are employed by scholars due to the diversity of their inclinations and tendencies. For instance, one meaning of daʿwah is to convey the guidance of God to His creations based on the Holy Qurʾan, the Hadith (Prophetic Tradition), and what has been traced to the Prophet and his successors.[5] A second meaning refers to the science of recognizing various technical methods in conveying the dogma, law, and ethics of Islam.[6] A third meaning is that which refers to conveying the message of Islam to all people and guiding them to it through profession and actions, in every era and

---

[1] Al-Afrīqī, Ibn Manẓur, *Lisān al-ʿArab*, vol. 1, p. 986.
[2] Fairūzābādī, Majd ud-Dīn, *Al-Qāmūs al-Muḥīṭ*, vol. 4, p. 327.
[3] Al-Jawharī, Ismaʾīl, *Al-Ṣiḥāḥ*, vol. 6, p. 2337.
[4] Al-Rāghib al-Isfahānī, Ḥusayn, *Al-Mufradāt fī Gharīb al-Qurʾan.*
[5] Hāshim, Aḥmad ʿUmar, *Al-Daʿwah al-Islamiyyah: Manāhijuhā wa Maʿālimuhā*, p. 6.
[6] Ghallūsh, Aḥmad, *Al-Daʿwah al-Islamiyyah: Usūluhā wa Wasāʾiluhā*, p. 10.

place, through means that are compatible with their invitees' types and temporal contexts.[7]

Within the Arabic literature, we find that the term daʿwah may encompass a number of meanings as well. Among these, daʿwah is used to connote supplication:

﴿أُجِيبُ دَعْوَةَ الدَّاعِ إِذَا دَعَانِ﴾

> "I (God) listen to the prayer of every supplicant when he/she calls upon Me."[8]

A second meaning is an invitation:

﴿قَالَ رَبِّ إِنِّي دَعَوْتُ قَوْمِي لَيْلًا وَنَهَارًا﴾

> "He [Prophet Noah] said: My Lord, surely I have invited my people night and day."[9]

A third meaning is an inquiry:

﴿قَالُوا ادْعُ لَنَا رَبَّكَ يُبَيِّن لَّنَا مَا لَوْنُهَا﴾

> "They [the followers of Prophet Moses] said: Inquire from your Lord to clarify for us its color."[10]

A fourth meaning is to summon:

﴿لَّا تَجْعَلُوا دُعَاءَ الرَّسُولِ بَيْنَكُمْ كَدُعَاءِ بَعْضِكُم بَعْضًا﴾

> "Treat not the calling of the Messenger among yourselves like the calling of one of you to another."[11]

And:

﴿ثُمَّ إِذَا دَعَاكُمْ دَعْوَةً مِّنَ الْأَرْضِ إِذَا أَنتُمْ تَخْرُجُونَ﴾

---

[7] Ḥasan, Muḥammad Amīn, *Khaṣāʾiṣ al-Daʿwah al-Islamiyyah*, p. 17.
[8] Qur'an, Sūrah al-Baqarah (2), verse 186.
[9] Qur'an, Sūrah Nūḥ (71), verse 5.
[10] Qur'an, Sūrah al-Baqarah (2), verse 69.
[11] Qur'an, Sūrah al-Nūr (24), verse 63.

"Then when He calls you by a single call from the earth, you will come forth [from your grave]."[12]

Relevant to our discussion in this work is that daʿwah connotes an invitation. However, this invitation is one that is of a special type and includes specific qualities and characteristics. The Qurʾan states:

﴿ٱدْعُ إِلَىٰ سَبِيلِ رَبِّكَ بِٱلْحِكْمَةِ وَٱلْمَوْعِظَةِ ٱلْحَسَنَةِ وَجَٰدِلْهُم بِٱلَّتِى هِىَ أَحْسَنُ﴾

"Invite to the way of your Lord with wisdom and beautiful preaching, and argue with them in ways that are best and most gracious."[13]

And:

﴿وَلْتَكُن مِّنكُمْ أُمَّةٌ يَدْعُونَ إِلَى ٱلْخَيْرِ وَيَأْمُرُونَ بِٱلْمَعْرُوفِ وَيَنْهَوْنَ عَنِ ٱلْمُنكَرِ﴾

"Let there arise out from among you a band of people inviting to all that is good, enjoining what is right and forbidding what is wrong." [14]

Thus, the argument is that this daʿwah (invitation) is one which is based on beautiful words, as well as one which is coupled with actions.

The term tablīgh linguistically refers to the act of conveyance or transmission. The noun is *bulūgh*. *Bulūgh*, *iblāgh*, or *tablīgh* all connote reaching a certain objective, whether spatial, temporal, or abstract.[15]

In the context of a spatial destination, the Qurʾan states:

﴿وَلَا تَحْلِقُوا رُءُوسَكُمْ حَتَّىٰ يَبْلُغَ ٱلْهَدْىُ مَحِلَّهُۥ﴾

---

[12] Qurʾan, Sūrah al-Rūm (30), verse 25.
[13] Qurʾan, Sūrah al-Naḥl (16), verse 125.
[14] Qurʾan, Sūrah Āle Imrān (3), verse 104.
[15] *Al-Mufradāt*. Also see *Lisān al-ʿArab*.

"And do not shave your heads until the offering arrives at the place of sacrifice."[16]

In the temporal context, the Qur'an states:

﴿حَتَّىٰ إِذَا بَلَغَ أَشُدَّهُ وَبَلَغَ أَرْبَعِينَ سَنَةً﴾

"Until when he reaches the age of full strength and attains forty years."[17]

In the context of abstract or incorporeal issues, the Qur'an states:

﴿قَدْ بَلَغْتَ مِن لَّدُنِّي عُذْرًا﴾

"You have received full excuse from my side."[18]

Conventionally, tablīgh refers to the transmission and conveyance of Divine guidance to the people. Thus, among the most important examples in the Qur'an, God states:

﴿يَا أَيُّهَا الرَّسُولُ بَلِّغْ مَا أُنزِلَ إِلَيْكَ مِن رَّبِّكَ﴾

"O Messenger, deliver what has been revealed to you from your Lord."[19]

And:

﴿الَّذِينَ يُبَلِّغُونَ رِسَالَاتِ اللَّهِ﴾

"Those who convey the messages of God."[20]

And:

﴿مَّا عَلَى الرَّسُولِ إِلَّا الْبَلَاغُ﴾

---

16 Qur'an, Sūrah al-Baqarah (2), verse 196.
17 Qur'an, Sūrah al-Aḥqāf (46), verse 15.
18 Qur'an, Sūrah al-Kahf (18), verse 76.
19 Qur'an, Sūrah al-Mā'idah (5), verse 67.
20 Qur'an, Sūrah al-Ahẓab (33), verse 39.

> "And there is no responsibility upon the Messenger, but that he conveys."[21]

Therefore, it may be argued that tablīgh refers to the process of teaching people to embrace the tenants of faith and to practice its articles. The Qur'an has also employed synonymous terms, besides daʿwah and tablīgh, such as *irshād* (guidance to the right course)[22] and *tabshīr* (missionary work or evangelism)[23] to connote similar meanings.

The two terms, daʿwah and tablīgh, are used interchangeably in the Qur'an, the Prophetic Tradition, and the Arabic literature. However, in addition to what has been stated above, within the context and scope of this book, I will employ the term daʿwah to refer specifically to the process of educating and inviting non-Muslims to knowledge and awareness of Islam in the West. On the other hand, I will employ the term tablīgh to specify the process of preaching to and teaching the Muslim community in the West.

The Significance of Daʿwah and Tablīgh

Daʿwah and tablīgh occupy a paramount position within Islam, since they represent the means of correspondence between God and His creation. The preacher (*muballigh*) is considered to be a successor of the messenger of God. The Prophet states: "May God have mercy upon my successors."[24] Imam al-Ṣādiq states: "A person will come on the Day of Judgment while he has accumulated a mountain-load of good deeds. He will ask: 'How did I receive this, while I did not perform these deeds?' He will be told: 'This is your knowledge that you passed onto other people and it was put into practice'."[25]

Also regarding daʿwah, Imam ʿAlī narrates that when Prophet Moses asked the Lord: "What is the reward for someone who invites a

---

21 Qur'an, Sūrah al-Mā'idah (5), verse 99.
22 Qur'an, Sūrah al-Jinn (72), verse 2.
23 Qur'an, Sūrah al-Isrā (17), verse 105.
24 Al-Majlisī, Muḥammad Bāqir, *Biḥār al-Anwār*, vol. 2, p. 25.
25 Ibid, vol. 2, p. 18.

non-believing person to faith?" The Lord replied: "I permit him to intercede on the Day of Judgment for whomever he desires."[26]

Interestingly, the Islamic tradition accentuates that the virtue of seeking knowledge is in fact a means to a greater objective and that is the propagation and dissemination of this knowledge to others. This encourages seekers of knowledge to equip themselves with the right knowledge, tools, and manners regarding daʿwah and tablīgh.

Prophet Muḥammad states: "No merit has been given to people better than knowledge that has been disseminated."[27]

Imam ʿAlī states: "When the Messenger of God dispatched me to Yemen, he said to me: 'O ʿAlī, do not fight with anyone unless you invite him to Islam first. By the Lord, if God guides a single person through you, it is more rewarding for you than everything that the sun rises and sets upon'."[28]

Imam al-Riḍā states: "The Jurist is the one who emanates his goodness to people and saves them from their enemies and who provides them with the blessings of God and His satisfaction."[29]

Imam al-Ṣādiq states: "On the Day of Judgment, both the scholar [preacher] and the worshipper *(ʿābid)* will stand before God. It will be said to the worshipper: 'Set off,' and to the scholar-preacher: 'Stand and intercede for people whom you have guided.'"[30]

Imam al-Bāqir states: "The scholar [preacher] is like one who carries a torch for people and whoever sees his/her torch will receive goodness."[31]

These traditions are but a small portion of a vast body of literature and they serve to prove that the virtue of the scholar and his/her reward are based on his/her preaching, teaching, and guiding the people.

---

[26] Al-Ṣadūq, Muḥammad ibn ʿAlī, *Al-Amālī*, p. 277.
[27] *Biḥār al-Anwār*, vol. 2, p. 25.
[28] Al-Kulaynī, Muḥammad ibn Yaʿqūb, *Al-Kāfī*, v. 5, p. 36.
[29] *Biḥār al-Anwār*, vol. 2, p. 6.
[30] Ibid., vol. 2, p. 16.
[31] Ibid., vol. 2, p. 5.

The Objectives of Daʿwah and Tablīgh

Islam aims to establish a complete human being; one who is spiritually and ethically transformed and suitable to act as the vicegerent (*khalīfah*) of God on the earth. This objective lies at the heart of the Islamic message. As such, the more significant the content and objective of a message is, the more important the process of delivering it will be. Since the higher objectives of the Islamic faith are universal and all-encompassing in their scope, including the purification and happiness of people, daʿwah and tablīgh are in turn, tools to accomplish these objectives.

It is noteworthy however, that there are two important aspects of an Islamic faith. The first is illustrated through the ideological/theological foundations of the tradition, while the second rests on the mannerisms and interaction of its members. In other words, there is a theoretical component to an Islamic lifestyle, and there is also a practical component. Based on numerous years of experience and many studies which have been conducted in this field, it is safe to say that westerners, and especially Americans, are influenced far greater by the practical component of Islamic teachings and Muslims than they are by the theoretical or ideological component.

In a recent report by the Muslim Public Affairs Council (MPAC), analysts concluded that American Muslims have significantly high unfavorable ratings among the general American public. According to the report, a HuffPo/YouGov poll conducted in March 2015 suggested that not only did 55% of Americans hold unfavorable views of Islam and Muslims, but that 44% have no interest at all in even learning about Islam.[32] Furthermore, the report stated that "While a majority had negative views, few seemed to base those judgments on knowledge or on relationships with Muslims. Just 13% told HuffPost/YouGov that they 'understand the Islamic religion' either extremely well or very well. In addition, 30% said they know the faith 'moderately well.' Meanwhile, 16% of Americans said they work with Muslims and nearly

[32] http://www.huffingtonpost.com/2015/04/10/americans-islam-poll_n_7036574.html. Visited January 1, 2016.

one in four said they have a friend who is Muslim.'"[33] In other words, the vast majority of those who hold unfavorable views of Islam and Muslims in fact do not personally know a Muslim: only 25% said they personally knew a Muslim.[34]

Essentially, what this implies is that relationships, which are based on interactions between Muslims and non-Muslims, are very important in mitigating problems and unfavorable views of Muslims. This fact, then increases the responsibility of those who engage in daʿwah and tablīgh to be exemplary role models and fine examples for those whom they educate.

There are numerous Prophetic traditions which emphasize the significant role of a Muslim's manners, conduct, and interactions with others in the development of true faith. For example, Prophet Muḥammad states: "A (genuine) Muslim is one who people are immune from [the evil of] his/her tongue (words) and hand (actions)."[35] He also states: "You will not be able to accommodate people with your wealth, but you may accommodate them with your conduct."[36] Thus, not everyone is fit to undertake the extremely important task of daʿwah and tablīgh. Educators and preachers must be able to adopt the Islamic message of conduct before passing it on to others. I will revisit this idea in the upcoming sections.

Exploring the Qur'anic verses leads us to conclude that some of the most important objectives of preaching are:

a. To breathe new life into the souls and hearts of the people:

﴿يَا أَيُّهَا الَّذِينَ آمَنُوا اسْتَجِيبُوا لِلَّهِ وَلِلرَّسُولِ إِذَا دَعَاكُمْ لِمَا يُحْيِيكُمْ﴾

[33] Ibid.
[34] Ibid.
[35] Al-Hindī, ʿAlī ibn ʿAbd al-Malik al-Muttaqī, *Kanz al-ʿUmmāl*, Ḥadīth no. 17.
[36] *Biḥār al-Anwār*, v. 74, p. 384.

"O you who believe, respond to God and the Messenger when they call you to that which brings you life."37

b. To invite everyone to monotheism:

﴿وَلَقَدْ بَعَثْنَا فِي كُلِّ أُمَّةٍ رَّسُولًا أَنِ اعْبُدُوا اللَّهَ وَاجْتَنِبُوا الطَّاغُوتَ﴾

"And we sent to every nation a messenger [saying]: Worship God and avoid the false deity/deities,"[38]

c. To create awareness of the hereafter:

﴿أَفَحَسِبْتُمْ أَنَّمَا خَلَقْنَاكُمْ عَبَثًا وَأَنَّكُمْ إِلَيْنَا لَا تُرْجَعُونَ﴾

"Did you think that We created you aimlessly, and that to Us you will not return?"[39]

d. To give glad tidings and to warn:

﴿يَا أَيُّهَا النَّبِيُّ إِنَّا أَرْسَلْنَاكَ شَاهِدًا وَمُبَشِّرًا وَنَذِيرًا﴾

"O Prophet, surely We have sent you as a witness and as a bringer of good tidings and as a warner."[40]

e. To secure human purification, nurturance, and perfection:

﴿هُوَ الَّذِي بَعَثَ فِي الْأُمِّيِّينَ رَسُولًا مِّنْهُمْ يَتْلُو عَلَيْهِمْ آيَاتِهِ وَيُزَكِّيهِمْ وَيُعَلِّمُهُمُ الْكِتَابَ وَالْحِكْمَةَ﴾

"It is He who sent among the unlettered a Messenger from themselves reciting to them His verses and purifying them and teaching them the Book and wisdom."[41]

---

37 Qur'an, Sūrah al-Anfāl (8), verse 24.
38 Qur'an, Sūrah al-Naḥl (16), verse 36.
39 Qur'an, Sūrah al-Mo'minūn (23), verse 115.
40 Qur'an, Sūrah al-Aḥzāb (33), verses 45-46.
41 Qur'an, Sūrah al-Jumuʿah (62), verse 2.

f. To enjoin good and forbid evil:

﴿وَلْتَكُن مِّنكُمْ أُمَّةٌ يَدْعُونَ إِلَى الْخَيْرِ وَيَأْمُرُونَ بِالْمَعْرُوفِ وَيَنْهَوْنَ عَنِ الْمُنكَرِ﴾

"And let there be [arising] from you a nation inviting to [all that is] good, enjoining what is right and forbidding what is wrong." [42]

The Underpinnings of Daʿwah and Tablīgh

The underpinnings of daʿwah and tablīgh are composed of three essential components.[43] The first of these components is the subject of the message that is being propagated, which is based on the Qurʾan and the authentic traditions of the Holy Prophet and his Household and righteous companions. According to the Prophetic Tradition, narrated by Jābir: "The best of speech (ḥadīth) is the Book of God, and the best form of guidance is that which is brought forth by Prophet Muḥammad."[44] The Qurʾan also states:

﴿وَمَنْ أَصْدَقُ مِنَ اللَّهِ حَدِيثًا﴾

"And who is more truthful in speech than God?"[45]

And:

﴿وَنَزَّلْنَا عَلَيْكَ الْكِتَابَ تِبْيَانًا لِّكُلِّ شَيْءٍ﴾

"And We have sent down to you the Book as clarification for all things."[46]

Thus, the Book of God and the Prophetic Tradition (including that of the Imams) gathers all forms of guidance and virtue, and does not

42 Qurʾan, Sūrah Āle ʿImrān (3), verse 104.
43 Ahmad Umar Hashim, p. 5.
44 Ibn Ḥanbal, Aḥmad, *Musnad Aḥmad.*
45 Qurʾan, Sūrah al-Nisāʾ (4), verse 87.
46 Qurʾan, Sūrah al-Naḥl (16), verse 89.

contain any exaggeration or superstitions. It is also important to note that this textual tradition must be examined within the spatial and temporal contexts. This will elaborated on in later sections.

The second component is the preacher him/herself and their intellectual, moral, and practical characteristics. The personality, lifestyle, and manners of the preacher/educator impacts people more than one's speech. The preacher has the potential to become a perfect role model in the way one conducts their life. There are numerous Islamic traditions that accentuate the role played by the character and personality of the preacher/educator. The Qur'an states:

﴿يَا أَيُّهَا الَّذِينَ آمَنُوا لِمَ تَقُولُونَ مَا لَا تَفْعَلُونَ﴾

> "O you who believe, why do you say that what you do not do?"[47]

Imam al-Ṣādiq states: "Invite to us silently (without the use of your tongues)."[48] This tradition emphasizes the characters of honesty, truth, integrity, earnestness, transparency, and piety in the life and manners of the preacher.

Imam ʿAlī states: "I have never invited you to perform a good action, unless I myself was the first to perform it. And when I asked you to refrain from something, I was the first one to refrain from it."[49] Once again, we see here an emphasis on the practical adoption of an ethical lifestyle before commanding or encouraging others to do so.

The third component of the underpinnings of daʿwah and tablīgh is the characteristics and identity of the invitees. The identity, conditions, challenges, ailments, and needs of a society frame the subject matter of daʿwah and tablīgh. Thus, it is imperative for the preacher/educator to closely examine these factors in order to provide the most effective forms of education. People play a major role in the direction, navigation, and content of the education. I have alluded to the fact that daʿwah and tablīgh in the East may in some aspects, differ from its

---

[47] Qur'an, Sūrah al-Ṣaff (61), verse 2.
[48] *Al-Kāfī*, v. 2, p. 78.
[49] Al-Raḍhī, Muḥammad ibn Ḥusayn al-Sharīf, *Nahj al-Balāghah*, sermon 175.

counterparts in the West. This is because the two societies are in many regards different in their needs, challenges, and ailments. In fact, even within one community, there are numerous layers to the needs and challenges of its components, and these layers will entail a specified message relevant to its audience.

The Peculiarities of Daʿwah and Tablīgh

Some scholars have summed up the distinctive features of Islamic daʿwah (in particular, how it is distinguished from other religious traditions) by stating that its origin is divine, its roadmap is prophetic, its path is middle, its perception of life is positive, its dealings with people is pragmatic, the means it seeks are ethical, its approach is versatile, its audience is universal, and its method of ruling is consultative. [50]

"Wisdom," "Good Advice," and "Harmonious Debate" as Guidelines

When the Qur'an discusses the topics of wisdom and good advice:

﴿ٱدْعُ إِلَىٰ سَبِيلِ رَبِّكَ بِٱلْحِكْمَةِ وَٱلْمَوْعِظَةِ ٱلْحَسَنَةِ ۖ وَجَٰدِلْهُم بِٱلَّتِى هِىَ أَحْسَنُ﴾

> "Call to the way of your Lord with wisdom and goodly exhortation, and have disputations with them in the best manner..."[51]

it presents a general framework for all legitimate, sensible, and open-minded discussions. Thus, one may pursue the approach that ends in wisdom and good advice. This includes practical advice, such as in the case of Prophet Abraham when employing logical inference:

﴿قَالَ بَلْ فَعَلَهُۥ كَبِيرُهُمْ هَٰذَا فَسْـَٔلُوهُمْ إِن كَانُوا۟ يَنطِقُونَ﴾

---

[50] ʿAbdul ʿAzīz, Jumʿah Amīn, *Al-Daʿwah, Qawāʾid wa Usūl*, p. 30.
[51] Qur'an, Sūrah al-Naḥl (16), verse 125.

"He [Abraham] said: The biggest one [idol] committed it, so ask them if they are able to speak."[52]

Similarly, Prophet Moses and Prophet Jesus introduced the approach of miracles, through wisdom (e.g. Prophet Moses and the sorcerers) and as a result, were successful:

﴿وَأُلْقِيَ السَّحَرَةُ سَاجِدِينَ قَالُوا آمَنَّا بِرَبِّ الْعَالَمِينَ رَبِّ مُوسَىٰ وَهَارُونَ﴾

"The sorcerers prostrated themselves. They said: We believe in the Lord of the worlds; the Lord of Prophet Moses and Aaron."[53]

The Qur'an also employs the approach of parables.[54]

According to ʿAllāmah al-Ṭabāṭabā'ī in his commentary of the Qur'ān, *al-Mīzān*, the last Prophet was commanded to preach based on the three tools of wisdom: good advice, and harmonious debate.

Al-Ṭabāṭabā'ī defines wisdom as "the evidence that produces certainty and does not bear suspicion, weakness, or ambiguity;" good advice as "the expression that draws inspiration and tenderness of the heart;" and harmonious debate as "the evidence that is employed to twist the antagonist from his insistence and argument."[55]

Furthermore, al-Ṭūsī in his commentary of the Qur'ān *al-Tibyān*, elaborates on these concepts - "Debating with people according to their capacity, based on the hadith: 'We, the community of the prophets, have been instructed to address people according to their mental capacities.'"[56]

Thus, al-Ṭabāṭabā'ī states that the combination of these three techniques constitutes the art of speech and oration. Interestingly

---

[52] Qur'an, Sūrah al-Anbiyā' (21), verse 63.
[53] Qur'an, Sūrah al-Aʿrāf (7), verses 120-122.
[54] Qur'an, Sūrah al-Baqarah (2), verse 26.
[55] Al-Ṭabā'tabā'ī, Sayyid Muḥammad Ḥusayn, *Al-Mīzān fi Tafsīr al-Qur'an*, v. 12, p. 303.
[56] Al-Ṭūsī, Muḥammad ibn Ḥasan, *Al-Tibyān fi Tafsīr al-Qur'an*, vol. 6, p. 440.

enough, al- Ṭabātabāʾī further elaborates that God's condition of advice being "good" means that there is some advice that is not good; conditioning debates being "better" means that some debates are not good, or they are good but not the best.[57]

Thus, according to these definitions, daʿwah requires the ability of deduction or presentation of argument according to sound logic, and aims to galvanize people's minds and penetrate their hearts. That is indeed a God-given quality:

﴿وَمَن يُؤْتَ الْحِكْمَةَ فَقَدْ أُوتِيَ خَيْرًا كَثِيرًا﴾

"And whoever is given wisdom has been given an abundance of goodness."[58]

Also, the Qurʾan states:

﴿وَلَقَدْ آتَيْنَا لُقْمَانَ الْحِكْمَةَ﴾

"And We bestowed wisdom upon Luqmān."[59]

According to *al-Kāfī*, Hishām ibn al-Ḥakam narrates from Imam Mūsā ibn Jaʿfar that the meaning of wisdom in this verse is: "comprehension and reason."[60]

Some scholars distinguish between wisdom and advice, stating that wisdom refers to the process of introducing a topic to someone who was unaware, while advice aims at reminding and raising attention to someone who was aware, but was heedless or had forgotten.[61]

Thus, wisdom, thus, aims at combatting ignorance, while advice aims at combatting forgetfulness. In other words, wisdom is to instill an idea, while advice is to stimulate reflection. While wisdom may be extracted from any source,[62] advice is profoundly impacted by the

---

[57] *Al-Mīzān fī Tafsīr al-Qurʾan*, v. 12, p. 304.
[58] Qurʾan, Sūrah al-Baqarah (2), verse 269.
[59] Qurʾan, Sūrah Luqmān (31), verse 12.
[60] *Al-Kāfī*, v. 1, p. 16.
[61] *Asālīb al-Tablīgh*, p. 114.
[62] Ibn Abī Shaybah, *Al-Muṣannaf*, vol. 7 p. 204; Abu Nuʿaym, *Ḥilyat al-Awliyāʾ*, vol. 5 p. 376.

personality and character of the preacher. This notion confirms the popular saying: "What originates from the heart enters the heart, and what originates from the mouth does not exceed the ears."

Daʿwah and Tablīgh in Various Religions

Daʿwah and tablīgh are not exclusive to the Islamic faith. We find that even among various other religious traditions, daʿwah and tablīgh are integral and serve vital roles in the religions' survival and success.

The general definition to the terms daʿwah and tablīgh may be missionary work or evangelism. Thus, a missionary is a member of a religious group sent into an area to conduct evangelical work or ministries of service, such as education, literacy, social justice, health care and economic development.

The word "mission" originates from the sixteenth century when the Jesuits sent members abroad, derived from the Latin *missionem* (nom. missio), meaning "act of sending" or *mittere*, meaning "to send."[63]

This word was used in light of its biblical usage; in the Latin translation of the Bible, Christ used this word when he sent the disciples to preach in his name. The term is most commonly used for Christian missions, but can be used for any creed or ideology.

Roman Catholic Missionary Work across the Globe

During the Age of Discovery and European global exploration, the Roman Catholic Church established a number of missions in the Americas and in other colonies through the Augustinians, Franciscans, and Dominicans in order to spread Christianity in the New World and to convert the Native Americans and other indigenous people. At about the same time, missionaries such as Francis Xavier (1506-1552), as well as other Jesuits, Augustinians, Franciscans, and Dominicans started moving into Asia and the Far East. The Portuguese sent missionaries into Africa.

---

63 http://www.merriam-webster.com/dictionary/mission. Visited January 1, 2016.

Contemporary Catholic Missionary Work

A lot of the contemporary Catholic missionary work has undergone profound changes since the Second Vatican Council of 1962-1965, and has become explicitly conscious of social justice issues and the dangers of cultural imperialism or economic exploitation disguised as religious conversion. Contemporary Christian missionaries argue that working for justice forms a constitutive part of preaching the Gospel, and they observe the principles of enculturation in their missionary work.

Early Protestant Missionaries

Early Protestant missionaries ministered to the Algonquin natives who lived in lands claimed by representatives of the Massachusetts Bay Colony in the early seventeenth century. Quaker "publishers of truth" visited Boston and other mid-seventeenth century colonies but were not always well received.

Modern Christian Missionary Work

With a dramatic increase in efforts since the 20th century, and a strong push since the Lausanne I: The International Congress on World Evangelization in Switzerland in 1974, modern evangelical groups have focused efforts on sending missionaries to every ethnic group in the world. While this effort has not yet been completed, increased attention has brought larger numbers of people distributing Bibles, Jesus videos, and establishing evangelical churches in more remote areas.

Internationally, the focus for many years in the later part of the 20th century was on reaching every "people group" with Christianity by the year 2000.

Bill Bright's leadership with Campus Crusade, the Southern Baptist International Mission Board, The Joshua Project, and others brought about the need to know who these "unreached people groups" are and how those wanting to tell about the Christian God and share a

Christian Bible could reach them. The focus for these organizations transitioned from a "country focus" to a "people group focus."[64]

Missionary Work in the Mormon Church

The Church of Jesus Christ of Latter-Day Saints (LDS Church) has an active missionary program. Young men between the ages of 18 and 25 are encouraged to prepare themselves to serve a two year, self-funded (often subsidized by the LDS Church), full-time proselytizing mission. Young women who desire to serve as missionaries can serve starting at the age of 19, for one and a half years. Retired couples also have the option of serving a mission.

Missionaries typically spend two weeks in a Missionary Training Center (or two to three months for those learning a new language) where they study the scriptures, learn new languages when applicable, prepare themselves to teach the Gospel of Jesus Christ, and learn more about the culture and the people among whom they will be spending time with.

Missionaries and Judaism

Despite some inter-Testamental Jewish missionary activity, contemporary Judaism states clearly that missionary activities are mostly taboo. Modern Jewish teachers repudiate proselytization of Gentiles in order to convert them. The reason for this is that Gentiles already have a complete relationship with God via the Noahidic covenant (The laws of Noah); there is therefore no need for them to become Jewish, which requires more work from them. In addition, Judaism espouses a concept of "quality" not "quantity." It is more important in the eyes of Jews to have converts who are completely

---

[64] From "What is a People Group?" by Dr. Orville Boyd Jenkins: A "people group" is an ethnolinguistic group with a common self-identity that is shared by the various members. There are two parts to that word: ethno and linguistic. Language is a primary and dominant identifying factor of a "people group". But there are other factors that determine or are associated with ethnicity.

committed to observing Jewish law, than to have converts who will violate the Abrahamic covenant into which they have been initiated.

Jewish religious groups encourage "Outreach" to Jews. The outreach, or *kiruv* movements, encourage Jews to become more knowledgeable and observant of Jewish law. People who become more observant are known as *baalei teshuva.* "Outreach" is done worldwide, by organizations such as Chabad Lubavitch, Aish Hatorah, Ohr Somayach, and Partners in Torah. There are also many such organizations in the West.

Members of the American Reform movement began a program to convert the non-Jewish spouses of its intermarried members to Judaism and non-Jews who have an interest in Judaism. Their rationale is that so many Jews were lost during the Holocaust that newcomers must be sought out and welcomed. This approach has been repudiated by Orthodox and Conservative Jews as unrealistic and pose to be a danger. They say that these efforts make Judaism seem to be an easy religion to join and observe, when in reality being Jewish involves many difficulties and sacrifices.

Daʿwah and Tablīgh Achievements in Various Religions

Among the various religious groups in the West, one may notice a great deal of significant achievements in various political, social, and religious dimensions. Following is a brief survey of some of the most important achievements and accomplishments of various religious groups.

The Catholic Church

Catholics make up approximately 24% of the population of America, making them the largest religious group in the nation.[65] According to the 2013 Annual Survey of the Catholic Charities USA (CCUSA) Service (the largest Catholic organization in America), Catholic Charities agencies and affiliates report that 2,759 local Catholic Charities service sites provided help and created hope for 9,035,223

---

[65] http://religions.pewforum.org/reports. Visited January 1, 2016.

unduplicated clients in 2013. Altogether, Catholic Charities agencies and affiliates reported providing client services over 17 million times, ranging from fulfilling basic needs for clothing and shelter to developing life skills such as financial literacy.[66]

In financial terms, Catholic Charities agencies and affiliates spent over $4.3 billion in 2013 on their services. Their agencies are composed of over 60,000 staff members and 277,000 volunteers.[67] All of this is in addition to the social justice committees, soup kitchens, food pantries, and other similar programs organized independently by thousands of Catholic parishes each year.

Furthermore, all of this excludes Catholic universities, which mainly provide higher education; hospitals, which are categorized separately from social services; and groups that focus on overseas work.

The Jesus Christ Church of Latter-Day Saints (Mormons)

Members of the Jesus Christ Church of Latter-Day Saints, also known as Mormons, make up approximately 1.7% of the American population.[68] Although a very small group, Mormons have had a great impact on the American society and continue to excel in various aspects of American life.

Throughout most of the 20th and 21st centuries, Mormons have aggressively pursued the most advanced education possible, understood their lives in terms of overcoming obstacles, and eagerly served their surrounding societies.

For Mormons, family is of supernatural importance, as well as will-planning and investing for future generations. Mormons are devoted to community, store and save as a hedge against future hardship, and esteem work as a religious calling. They are greatly involved in philanthropy and humanitarian work across the world, including America.

---

[66] http://www.scribd.com/doc/239473494/2013-Annual-Survey-Overview. Visited January 1, 2016.
[67] Ibid.
[68] http://religions.pewforum.org/reports. Visited January 1, 2016.

One of the interesting points about Mormons is that according to their website, "Two tenets of humanitarian aid define Humanitarian Services:

1) 100% of every dollar donated is used to help those in need without regard to race, religion, or ethnic origin; and

2) Humanitarian Services help people attain self-sufficiency so they can be self reliant long after Humanitarian Services departs."[69]

As of January 2014, the LDS Church had over 80,000 missionaries worldwide and over 10,000 Welfare Services Missionaries.

The Jews

The Jewish population in the United States of America is estimated at 5-6 million, rivaling the Mormons at about 1.7% of the American population.[70]

Interestingly, Jews make up one of the most powerful minorities, especially in America. They have high levels of educational attainment; and most of them are college graduates (58%), including 28% who say they have earned a post-graduate degree. By comparison, 29% of U.S. adults say they graduated from college, including 10% who have a post-graduate degree.[71]

Furthermore, there are currently 3,727 Jewish places of worship and approximately 4,000 Jewish Rabbis, as well as over 100 Jewish universities and seminaries, and 800 Jewish schools in America.[72]

---

[69] http://www.ldsphilanthropies.org/humanitarian-services.html. Visited January 1, 2016

[70] http://religions.pewforum.org/reports. Visited January 1, 2016.

[71] http://www.pewforum.org/2013/10/01/jewish-american-beliefs-attitudes-culture-survey/. Visited January 1, 2016.

[72] Al-Qazwini, Sayed Moustafa, *Tajribātī fil Gharb*, p. 57.

Chapter Two: The United States of America

Religious Identity in the United States

Approximately two centuries ago, while traveling across America, the French political thinker and historian Alexis de Tocqueville recognized the pivotal role of religion in shaping American life. He wrote: "This civilization is the result ... of two quite distinct ingredients, which anywhere else have often ended in war, but which Americans have succeeded somehow to meld together in wondrous harmony; namely, the spirit of religion and the spirit of liberty."[1] Tocqueville found that religion and freedom in America were "intimately united," whereas in his country of origin, France, "the spirit of religion and the spirit of freedom seemed to march in opposite directions."[2]

It is noteworthy that freedom plays an important role when coupled with religion. There may be instances when religion and freedom are considered contradictory forces – when religion is perceived as a restrictive force and freedom a liberating force. In some societies, the imposition of religious rulings and laws upon the masses has led to negative consequences, including anti-religious fervor and the outright rejection of religious and/or theistic beliefs. On the other hand, the restriction of freedom in practicing religion may also encourage heightened religious extremism on part of those who consider religion to be vital for their lives. In the case of the United States, the Constitution's protection of religious freedoms as well as its prohibition of establishment of religion (separation of church and

---

[1] Pew Forum on Religion and Public Life, *U.S. Religious Landscape Survey,* February 1, 2008.

[2] Eck, Diana, *A New Religious America,* p. 43.

state), have in fact paved the way for religious identity and practice to flourish.[3]

According to the Pew Forum on Religious and Public Life, religion is a very important part of the American identity: 92% of Americans believe in the existence of God, 74% believe in life after death, 56% say religion is very important in their lives, 54% attend religious services fairly regularly (at least once or twice per month), and 58% say they pray every day.[4]

The role of spirituality and religion in the United States and in the lives of Americans is a matter of fact. Religion remains a powerful force in both the private and public lives of most Americans. Americans continue to search for answers to various challenges and questions that they have through religion. The Pew Forum suggests that almost half of the American adults have converted from one religious tradition to another, with a large majority converting before the age of 36.[5] This suggests that dynamism and constant movement characterizes the American religious marketplace.

Another important factor to note is that most Americans have a non-dogmatic approach to faith and religion. According to Diana Eck, "Americans, on the whole, have a high degree of religious identification...and yet a very low level of religious literacy."[6] A strong majority of Americans (70%) do not believe that their religion is the only way to salvation. Almost the same percentage believe that there is more than one true way to interpret the teachings of their own religion.[7] This factor, coupled with the constitutional right of freedom of religion, has not only led to religious diversity in the general public, but also within families with members adhering to various religious traditions and faiths. We find in some cases that within one nuclear family, there are one or more religious traditions and denominations

---

[3] See the First Amendment to the Constitution of the United States: http://www.archives.gov/exhibits/charters/bill_of_rights_transcript.html. Visited January 1, 2016.

[4] *U.S. Religious Landscape Survey*, pp. 6-12.

[5] http://www.pewforum.org/2009/04/27/faith-in-flux/. Visited January 1, 2016.

[6] *A New Religious America*, p. 70.

[7] *U.S. Religious Landscape Survey*, p. 4.

represented by the various family members. According to the Pew Forum, among people who are married, nearly four-in-ten (37%) are married to a spouse with a different religious affiliation (this includes Protestant Christians who are married to another Protestant from a different denomination).[8]

Finally, the perceptions of Americans vis-à-vis religion may be categorized into four groups:

1. The first group completely rejects faith and identifies itself with atheism;
2. The second group is characterized by those who identify themselves as secular, distinguishing between private and public forms of religious displays;
3. The third group is the religiously committed and practicing - those who believe in the strong impact of religion in public and private life;
4. Finally, the fourth group is characterized by the religiously unaffiliated - they experience a spiritual void, but are on a quest for spiritual satisfaction. Each of these groups represent an important force in the American religious landscape.

Social Identity in the United States

In his seminal work on Islam in America entitled *Journey into America*, Akbar Ahmed suggests that the nature of American identity is a complicated mix of historical, ethnic, sociological, and emotional dimensions, and is based on three distinct but overlapping identities: primordial, pluralist, and predator.[9]

Ahmed argues that the primordial identity, which is characterized by the early settlers' aim of survival and creation of a Christian society, serves as the foundation for the other two identities.[10] While some of the early settlers' actions were based on excessive religious zeal and fear, Ahmed writes, "others, who still clung onto their Christian faith,

[8] http://religions.pewforum.org/reports. Visited January 1, 2016.
[9] Ahmed, Akbar, *Journey into America*, p. 45.
[10] Ibid.

hoped to create a society in which everyone could live according to his or her faith and under the rule of law."[11] This understanding would develop into what Ahmed calls the pluralist identity.

On the other hand, there were also those who considered the new land given to them by God, and with time, early colonists became overly confident, built new settlements, and began to prey on the weaker natives with impunity. Ahmed states, "This aggressive impulse generated arrogance" that "made it easy to demonize and destroy the enemy," and resulted in the formation of the predator identity.[12]

Ahmed further argues that this identity resulted in the adoption of zero tolerance towards the natives and others, for the settlers "lived in constant fear of natives wiping them out, and this emotion embedded itself deep in their psyche, leading them to demand a solution that would remove the threat permanently ... within half a century of the *Mayflower's* landing, the native tribes would be decimated in New England."[13] Thus, the central dynamic of American society may be viewed through the tensions that arose between these identities.

American identity has been profoundly shaped by the English. The English introduced the idea of limiting the authority of a ruler through the Magna Carta Libertatum, the Great Charter of Freedoms issued in 1215.[14]

Furthermore, Ahmed argues, while some English settlers retained respect and loyalty to the British monarchy, "most had said goodbye to their country and their king. In America, they would be judged and tested as individuals. Even their links with the church would loosen and weaken."[15]

In time, Americans would adopt a new kind of religion, what sociologists like Robert Bellah have called a "civil religion."[16]

---

[11] Ibid.
[12] Ibid.
[13] Ibid: p. 51.
[14] Ibid: p. 53.
[15] Ibid.
[16] Bellah, Robert, "Civil Religion in America," *Daedalus, Journal of the American Academy of Arts and Sciences* 96 (Winter 1967), pp. 1-21.

Additionally, in the 18th century, while American identity was being hotly contested, the Founding Fathers of the United States, such as George Washington, Thomas Jefferson, Thomas Madison, and Benjamin Franklin, were discussing issues such as freedom, liberty, and democracy.[17]

Social Tendencies of Americans

Americans exhibit many social tendencies and uphold a number of significant core values. Among these values, many are positive and contribute to the well-being of society and all citizens.

For example, Americans exhibit a strong work ethic, and for them, working hard underlies progress and success. Laziness or idleness is generally frowned upon, and leisure is seen as a natural reward for hard work.

Americans are action and achievement oriented. There is strong emphasis on "getting things done" through detailed goal setting, planning, and action.

Competition is also important in American society. Students and the youth are encouraged from a young age to be competitive in their education and work. For Americans, being "number 1" is very important.

They are also well-known for emphasizing volunteerism; and they generally exhibit a culture of collaboration and cooperation, for they believe in helping others (albeit as a personal choice, not a communal expectation). Thus, philanthropy is admired in the American society, and the Americans are highly philanthropic: according to a recent report, every year more than $350 billion is handed out by American individuals and organizations to various charitable causes; rates of giving are two- to five-times higher in the United States than in comparable nations.[18]

However, there are other values and tendencies that may lead to negative consequences, both to individuals and to the society. Among

---

[17] *Journey into America*, p. 58.
[18] http://www.philanthropyroundtable.org/almanac. Visited January 1, 2016.

the most important of these tendencies are individualism and materialism.

Individualism here refers to the idea that each human being is unique and free to pursue his/her private and individual satisfactions and objectives independently of others. In turn, this sense of individualism entails promoting the well-being of an individual and takes precedence over social well-being. Essentially, individualism stems from a high degree of freedom which is promoted in American society. Thus, we find that Americans emphasize their right to make their own decisions in life, and should not be restricted by social, governmental, or religious restrictions. A clear example of this type of logic may be found in the abortion debate, where proponents of legalizing abortion are labeled "pro-choice."

Another important social tendency among Americans is materialism. Of course, it may be argued that most Americans would not admit to being materialistic, as this term implies a negative connotation. They may consider their acquisition and dependence on material possessions as a "natural" part of their lives – they work hard, earn an income, and freely spend their income on things that they desire, including material possessions – what is commonly referred to as pursuing the "American Dream."

In any case, generally, Americans are materialistic and deeply value their material possessions. This phenomenon may be clearly seen when analyzing American trends in consumerism. For example, reports suggest that an average American will drain as many resources as 35 natives of India and consume 53 times more goods and services than someone from China.[19] According to some estimates, the average credit card debt per American household is over $15,000.[20]

Many Americans are focused on narrow personal interests and material gains. Contrary to popular thought, these materialistic and individualistic tendencies are a cause of distress for many Americans.

---

[19] http://www.scientificamerican.com/article/american-consumption-habits/. Visited January 1, 2016.

[20] http://www.usatoday.com/story/money/personalfinance/2014/03/24/20-ways-we-blow-our-money/6826633/. Visited January 1, 2016.

Many psychological studies have shown that materialism is not associated with happiness, but rather with dissatisfaction, depression, anxiety, anger, isolation, and alienation.[21] Interestingly enough we find that many Americans realize the negative consequences of living individualistic and materialistic lives, and as such, embark on quests to find meaning and purpose in their lives. As a result, some Americans turn to Islam for answers on how to overcome the various challenges that they face in their daily lives.

[21] http://ije.oxfordjournals.org/content/35/2/252.full. Visited January 1, 2016.

Chapter Three: History and Rise of Islam in the United States of America

The history and rise of Islam and Muslims in the United States is usually discussed in the context of post-twentieth century immigration, the civil rights movement (African-American Muslims), and more recent events that have transpired domestically and globally. However, during the last two decades of the twentieth century, a growing body of scholarly work has begun to emerge in the West that calls into question much of the conventional wisdom and thoughts on American history. One of the important areas of focus is the history of Islam and Muslims in America.

According to Jerald F. Dirks in his book *Muslims in American History*, he writes: "The history of Islam in America can be traced back through the centuries for what appears to be well over 1,000 years."[1]

Specifically, the interrelationships of Muslims and America stretch back to the ninth century when the first documented voyage took place from Muslim Andalusia (contemporary Spain and Portugal) to the Americas.[2]

This relationship continued through pre-Columbian voyages from Muslim Andalusia, Africa, and as some have suggested, the ʿUthmānī Empire as well.[3] Muslims sailed with Christopher Columbus and were also integral parts of later Spanish explorations.

From Africa, the sixteenth to nineteenth century slave trade brought millions of Muslims to the shores of America.

In colonial America, there existed a Muslim group known as the Melungeons, who were descendants of Muslims from mixed ethnic

---

[1] Dirks, Jerald F., *Muslims in American History, A Forgotten Legacy*, p. 10.
[2] Ibid, p. 11.
[3] Ibid.

backgrounds and centered primarily in the Appalachian region. According to researchers, many of the aforementioned groups seems to have intermarried with and occasionally absorbed into American Indian (native) tribes, and identifiable Muslim names can even be found from Cherokee Indians well into the nineteenth century.[4]

The late nineteenth century witnessed the first waves of modern Muslim immigration to the United States from the Arab provinces of the ʿUthmānī Empire.[5] Finally, successive waves of Muslim immigration from various parts of the Islamic world continued throughout the twentieth century.[6]

Muslim presence in contemporary America is composed mainly of recent immigrants, converts to Islam, and second and third and some fourth-generation Muslims. It must be noted that in some cases, there is an overlap between these groups (for example, some Muslims are immigrants and converts; others may be second or third generation Muslims whose parents or grandparents were converts, and so on).

The first group of Muslims are the immigrants. Most Muslims in America today are immigrants (63%); almost half (45%) of which arrived in the United States since 1990.[7] The immigrants come from a wide range of countries across the Muslim world. Some chose to migrate purely for economic reasons and a chance to establish a better life for themselves and their families. Among this group, many were poverty-stricken and did not possess academic degrees. This group of immigrants did not necessarily have an impact on American society. Rather, some segments of this group may very well have been influenced by American society and culture, sometimes very negatively. Others seemed to do well-off in their pursuit of the "American Dream."

Another group among the immigrants were the students that intended on pursuing their educational goals and careers. They

---

[4] Ibid, pp. 12-13.
[5] Ibid, p. 13.
[6] Ibid.
[7] http://www.people-press.org/2011/08/30/a-portrait-of-muslim-americans/. Visited January 1, 2016.

studied, interacted, graduated, and remained in society. Some were and continue to be religiously committed, while others were non-religious. Among the committed, some students came together and established national Muslim organizations - such as the Islamic Circle of North America, Islamic Society of North America, Muslim Student Association, Muslim Group of USA and Canada, and others, that remain very active even until today.

A third group of Muslims sought immigration for political reasons (refugees, asylum seekers); some remained poor, while others were or became influential and continue to be influential thinkers, academics, policy makers, and leaders.

The second group of Muslims is those who comprise the second and third generation. These are the progeny of Muslim immigrants or converts who were born and raised in America. They make up a small, but growing minority of the Muslim population in the country. Although many members among this group may admit to their ancestral cultures (e.g. Lebanese-American, Egyptian-American, etc.), this group identifies primarily with American culture and language. To the vast majority among this group, there is no contradiction whatsoever to being Muslim and American. They are well-established in society; some have become leaders in various sectors of society - including medicine, law, politics, entertainment, and scholarship. According to one report, 41 out of the 500 most influential Muslims in the world are American.[8]

Finally, converts make up about 23% of the Muslim community in the United States. According to some estimates, 91% of converts to Islam were born in the United States, and almost 59% of the converts to Islam are African-American.[9] Furthermore, a 55% majority of converts identify with Sunnī Islam and another quarter (24%) identify with no specific tradition. Only 6% of Muslim converts in America

---

[8] http://www.washingtonpost.com/national/on-faith/us-dominates-list-of-worlds500-most-influential-muslims/2012/11/28/27187f62-3999-11e2-9258-ac7c78d5c680_story.html. Visited January 1, 2016.

[9] http://www.pewresearch.org/daily-number/converts-to-Islam/. Visited January 1, 2016.

identify themselves as Shīʿa.[10] The following sections will further discuss the existence, role, and challenges of converts to Islam.

The Shīʿa in the United States of America

Most of the first Muslims to arrive to America were Sunnī. The Shīʿa Muslims, along with the Druzes and ʿAlawīs, began to arrive in more significant numbers during the end of the nineteenth century and beginning of the twentieth century.

Reports indicate that the first Shīʿa Muslims to migrate to the United States were of Lebanese origin, and they resided in the cities of Ross, North Dakota and Michigan City, Indiana in the year 1899.[11]

Shīʿa immigrants in Michigan City in the year 1900 were around 200 families, and they established their own institution in 1914 named "al-Badr al-Munīr," and subsequently their own mosque in 1924 in the same city.[12] Their activities increased between 1920 and 1930, and then many of them began to move to other areas such as Dearborn and Grand Rapids, Michigan.

Studies suggest that at least three passengers on the ship *Titanic*, which sank in the Atlantic Ocean in 1912, were Shīʿa from South Lebanon: Mrs. Fatima Masselmany was 17 years old when she survived the event and went on to live in Michigan City; but her cousins Mustafa Nasr and Yousif Wazli both drowned in the incident. Mrs. Masselmany moved to Dearborn and lived there until she passed away in 1971.[13]

Among the first Shīʿa religious leaders who moved to the United States were Sayed Safi al-Din and Sheikh Muḥammad Jawad Chirri who came from Lebanon in 1949.[14]

The Shīʿa Muslim immigrants began to increase in number as they escaped the Ottoman rule in Lebanon in the nineteenth century. From 1900 to 1974, immigrants from Lebanon began to join their families, and after 1922, Shīʿa Muslims from the Indian Subcontinent and Iran

---

10 Ibid.

11 Takim, Liyakat, *Shi'ism in America*, p. 12.

12 Ibid, p. 13.

13 Ibid.

14 Ibid.

began to migrate to America, most of them comprising of laborers and working class people, especially as the Ford Motor Company rode to prominence. Henry Ford began to pay them competitive wages: he would pay $5 a day, which was a considerable income in 1913.

After World War I and the fall of the Ottoman Empire, from 1918 to 1922, the second wave of Arabs and Muslims began to immigrate to the United States, especially to Michigan. The collapse of the economy in their regions, as well as an increase in unemployment, food scarcity, and spread of disease that followed World War I added to the number of migrants.

The division of the Arab Muslim countries into British and French colonies led to increased migration from villages and towns across Lebanon and other Middle Eastern countries.

In the year 1940, the Shīʿa of Dearborn purchased a building from a bank and transformed it into the "Hāshimī Hall" to be the first social and religious center in the area. The gatherings held there would bring together a mix of Shīʿa and Sunnīs.[15]

Subsequently in 1963, the first Shīʿa Islamic center was established in the same city under the name of the "Islamic Center of America," and religious functions were held there. Many scholars and educators came there to teach and guide the masses, and after forty years the center relocated to a newly built building. It is now considered to be one of the biggest mosques in America. Almost twenty Shīʿa Islamic institutions have been established in the Dearborn area, serving the Lebanese, Iraqi, and Pakistani communities, as well as others.

Unofficial statistics suggest that about half a million Arabs live in the greater Detroit area, most of which are Lebanese, and there are also Iraqi Christians, Iraqi Shīʿa, Yemenis, and other communities.[16]

In 1953, the Government of the United States established an immigration quota for each Arab and Muslim country. Consequently, Shīʿa immigrants from the Middle East and the Indian subcontinent began to migrate to America. Many of them were students, who were

---

[15] Ibid, p. 15.
[16] Ibid, p. 17.

expected to return to their countries after studying - but studies show that approximately two-thirds of the incoming students preferred to remain in the United States after completing their studies, rather than returning back.

Shīʿa Islam began to spread across America to cities such as New York and Chicago, and between 1950-1960, many Iranians arrived to study in the United States. As a result of the adjustment of the immigration quota during the presidency of Lyndon Johnson in 1965, which was to the benefit of the third world countries, the number of Muslim immigrants to the United States increased from 4% in 1968, to 10.5% in 1986.[17]

Many Muslims, among them Shīʿa, spread across the entire country, especially after the Islamic revolution in Iran in 1979, the Iran-Iraq war from 1980-1988, and after the first and second Gulf wars in 1991 and 2003 in Iraq. With the spread of the Shīʿa in America came the establishment of religious centers and mosques. Today, there are Shīʿa Islamic centers in more than 45 states, and others throughout the provinces of Canada.

It is estimated that about one-fifth of the Muslim population in the United States are Shīʿa.[18] Iranians form the largest Shīʿa group in the United States, estimated at 1 million, about half of which live in California.[19] The next largest concentration of the community Shīʿa are in Michigan, followed by New York, New Jersey, Texas, and Illinois.

Some unofficial reports indicate that there are about two hundred Shīʿa Islamic centers and mosques in America. Out of these, twenty-two centers are located in Southern California, and ten are in Northern California.

In America and Canada, there are about 150 Shīʿa preachers and educators, coming from different ethnicities and backgrounds, including: American, Canadian, Iraqi, Lebanese, Iranian, Indian, Pakistani, Arab, Afghani, and East African.

---

[17] Ibid, p. 21.
[18] Ibid, p. 23.
[19] Ibid, p. 27.

In addition to Islamic centers and mosques, the Shīʿa were able to establish various national organizations, which support political and civic activity inside the United States. One example is the Universal Muslim Association of America (UMAA), which held its 13th annual conference in 2015 in Chicago.

Shīʿa Muslims have also participated in the establishment of many websites concerning daʿwah, general Islamic education, and youth issues. They have succeeded in establishing satellite channels in multiple languages that aim to spread the message of Islam, the Prophet and his Ahlulbayt, and to further the understanding between Islamic schools of thought and divine religions.

Among the notable efforts of the Shīʿa in America is that of the youth. Among these efforts and activities are weekly youth sessions held in many centers and mosques, as well as youth camps that are held in California, Michigan, New York, and across Canada, which have a major influence in raising the youth in order to identify with their Muslim identity and to prepare them for the future. These camps have created many positive results, such as guiding some of the young participants to observe proper Islamic manners, and observe the ḥijāb, as well as conversion to Islam and social cohesion. These and other youth initiatives and activities have contributed to an increase in Islamic awareness and preparing them to carry out responsibilities in the social, political, civil, religious, and intellectual sectors in this country.

Living in America does not come free from hardships and challenges for Muslims in general, and for Shīʿa Muslims specifically. Among these challenges is the interaction of Shīʿa youth with their Sunnī counterparts. This relationship has been characterized by tension in the last two decades, mostly as a result of the promotion of sectarianism from some Islamic countries who try to cause conflict between the two schools. Often, Shīʿa Muslims have been expelled and discriminated from gatherings and conferences, and even congregational and Friday prayers which take place at American universities.

Despite the attempts of leaders and scholars to diffuse these conflicts, their affects are still present at American universities and Islamic centers across the United States. As an example, in 1994, the Islamic Educational Center of San Diego was established. The reason was because a group of Shīʿa Muslims would pray and congregate at a Sunnī masjid in the same city, however, a sectarian conflict arose between the two groups. This lead to the expulsion of the Shīʿa group, which created a need to find their own place of worship, and by the grace of God, they were able to acquire a former church in the city of Lakeside in San Diego, and transform it into the first Shīʿa Islamic center in the city. This tension and conflict sometimes even extends to the prison system between Shīʿa and Sunnī inmates, and in some cases even leads to conflict resulting in legal cases before the judicial system.

Types of Muslim Immigrants: Assimilation, Integration, and Isolation

Recent decades have witnessed large numbers of Muslim immigrants to the West, in particular to Europe and the United States of America. For some people, immigration to the West has met positive outcomes, while for others immigration has had some negative ramifications. For many Muslim immigrants, adapting to a new way of life is a major challenge; however, not all immigrants have had the same experiences. Muslim immigrants to the United States of America can generally be categorized into three distinct groups: assimilationists, integrationists, and isolationists.

Assimilationists are those groups of immigrants who tend to fully immerse themselves into society, while leaving their unique linguistic, cultural, and even religious differences behind. According to Diana Eck, author of *A New Religious America*, "The most vivid image here is the melting pot, the crucible where differences dissolve into the common pot, adding their flavors but losing their forms."[20] Thus, many Muslim immigrants relinquish the most distinctive aspects of their

---

[20] *A New Religious America*, p. 54.

home culture to take on the Western culture. I have come across some individuals and families who, in the name of assimilation into American culture, have completely ceased their mother languages, cultures, and some who have also lost their Islamic religious identity as well.

According to a report by the Pew Research Center, Muslims in America have a retention rate of approximately 77% - therefore, approximately 23% of Muslims surveyed no longer identify with their Islamic childhood religion.[21]

The second type of immigrants is the integrationists. This group is represented by those who are able to maintain a balance between integrating into the various social, political, and economic aspects of American culture, while maintaining their distinctive cultural and religious identities. The twentieth century sociologist Horace Kallen depicts this group in the image of a symphony, not a melting pot: "America is a symphony orchestra, sounding not unison, but harmony, with all the distinctive tones of our many cultures."[22] It may be fair to suggest that the majority of Muslims in America today are well-integrated into the American society, and their everyday activities are very similar to the rest of the general public's. Furthermore, the vast majority fully retain their religious identities, as well as some portions of their native cultural and linguistic identities.

According to a Pew Research Center report, "Like U.S. Christians, many U.S. Muslims are highly religious. Fully 69% say that religion is very important in their lives, compared with 70% Christians. Almost half of both U.S. Muslims and U.S. Christians report attending worship services at least weekly."[23] Muslim immigrants in America realize that they can (and do) change many things, including their style of dress, their politics, and their economic status, but that they also have the right (and actively exercise it) to be different, not just in dress and

---

[21] http://www.pewforum.org/2015/05/12/americas-changing-religious-landscape/. Visited January 1, 2016.

[22] *A New Religious America*, p. 57.

[23] http://www.people-press.org/2011/08/30/a-portrait-of-muslim-americans/. Visited January 1, 2016.

public presentation, but in every other aspect of their lives, united only by participation in the common covenants of citizenship.

The third category of Muslim immigrants is the isolationists. This group engages in political, cultural, and social alienation by completely distancing themselves from all forms of integration in American society and culture. In some cases, isolationist immigrants deliberately avoid learning the English language, confine their children's education to learning and memorizing the Qur'an, and avoid applying for U.S. citizenship. The main reason for adoption of such a lifestyle is the assumed protection of their families and communities from the negative consequences of adopting Western culture and the preservation of their own cultural and religious identity.

One example of this group may be found in the city of Buffalo, New York. According to Akbar Ahmed in his elaborate study of Islam in America, the Muslim community of Dārul ʿUlūm Al-Madaniya, a boarding school for boys that trains future imams, consider themselves as the true champions of Islam in America and "reject American identity altogether as irrelevant to their lives."[24] During his visit to the school, Ahmed found that the children who were enrolled wore traditional Arab/Southeast Asian clothing (both inside and outside the school), spent their time learning only the Qur'an, Arabic, and Islamic law, and rarely any of the children interviewed had non-Muslim friends. School schedules and postings were all in Arabic and Urdu. Furthermore, when the school office staff was asked how the students coped with the "outside world," the reply was, "We teach them dīn [religion] only. As long as they keep the dīn, they will be okay on the outside."[25] When asked about what they thought of American identity, they were told: "We don't think about it."[26]

The Predicaments of Converts to Islam

Despite the rise of anti-Islamic sentiment and Islamophobia in America and elsewhere, there is a steady growth in the number of converts to

---

[24] *Journey into America*, p. 216.
[25] Ibid, p. 217.
[26] Ibid, p. 219.

Islam in America. In fact, Islam is the fastest growing religion in America, with significant growth stemming from conversion.[27] However, the issues and process surrounding conversion to Islam are not always without tension and problems. Before, during, and after embracing Islam, converts tend to face a number of challenges. While some of their problems (i.e. spiritual, religious) are resolved through their conversion, other challenges arise, such as those pertaining to social issues. For example, one problem many converts face is alienation and non-acceptance from their family and/or friends. The Muslim convert in the family begins to adopt various changes to normative customs and traditions that may not be familiar or comfortable for the rest of the family members.

One prevalent example is that of the dietary changes that occur with conversion. A Muslim convert and his/her family must now attempt to delicately respond to the preparation of meals: how to prepare halal meals, the sharing of a meal, the existence of alcohol in the home and on the dinner table, and issues pertaining to religious purity and impurity of the food, and items used in preparing the food are but a few examples.

Another major hurdle may be related to the observance of ḥijāb: parents, siblings, children, or other family members or friends may discourage (and sometimes prohibit) the Muslim female convert from observing ḥijāb.

On the other hand, converts may not receive full admission and acceptance into Muslim communities, especially those communities that are composed primarily of immigrants. Frequently, converts clash with the immigrant Muslim culture and community, facing drastic consequences. Many converts face difficulties in finding adequate and suitable friends and acquaintances. Furthermore, both male and female converts face immense challenges getting married within the Muslim community.

Many immigrant (and sometimes second and third generation) Muslim families continue to hold cultural baggage that eschews them

---

27 http://www.pewforum.org/2015/04/02/muslims/. Visited January 1, 2016.

from allowing family members to marry outside of their specific nationality, ethnicity, or race. Thus, converts encounter the dual challenges of losing their family members and friends, and not being able to replace this loss with Muslim friends and family members. This phenomenon undoubtedly causes immense social and psychological challenges for converts.

Additionally, most Islamic organizations have failed to provide a favorable environment for converts. As an example, one problem is the language barrier and native cultures and customs associated with various immigrant communities. Some centers, especially those that are Shīʿa, insist on conducting programs in their own native languages, such as Persian, Urdu, and Arabic. The vast majority of converts to Islam do not speak or understand these languages. Thus, converts are excluded from participating and benefitting from the programs held at these centers.

Conversely, some communities and Islamic centers attempt to dump lots of information and push for strict observance of rituals and customs upon converts, overwhelming them in the process. Sometimes, converts are enthusiastic about their new-found faith and dedicated to practicing Islam, but find that a community may be un-Islamic or non-observant. They may be discouraged or even shocked to witness unexpected behaviors. On the other hand, there are instances when the conversion is only verbal, with no genuine commitment to the religion. This is especially evident in some conversions with matrimonial and/or economic motivations.

Consequently, it is evident that converts to Islam in America face numerous challenges. In the following relevant sections, I will elaborate on some recommendations in order to help overcome various challenges faced by converts and their respective communities.

Islamophobia[28]

The United States of America is one of the most religiously diverse nations in the world today. Various reports estimate the Muslim population in America to be between 2.5 to 7 million, making up approximately 1-2% of the total American population.[29] Yet Islam continues to be one of the most misunderstood religions in America. According to the Pew Research Center, a large majority (65%) of Americans consider Islam to be very or somewhat quite different than their own religion. Furthermore, events and controversies related to Islam dominated U.S. press coverage of religion in 2010,[30] and 53% of Americans surveyed were "very concerned about the possibility of rising Islamic extremism in the U.S."[31]

Islamophobia is an undeniable reality in the American landscape. The industry of Islamophobia and anti-Muslim sentiments has been growing steadily since the terrorist attacks of September 11, 2001. According to the Council on American-Islamic Relations (CAIR), there currently exists at least 37 inner core groups and individuals, with a total revenue of approximately $120 million, whose primary purpose is to promote prejudice against and hatred of Islam and Muslims. Additionally, as of 2012, 78 legislation bills designed to vilify Islam have been introduced in 29 states and the United States Congress.[32]

---

[28] "Islamophobia" refers to the exaggerated fear, hatred, and hostility towards Islam and Muslims that is perpetuated by negative stereotypes resulting in bias, discrimination, and the marginalization and exclusion of Muslims from America's social, political, and civic life.

[29] The range of estimates is wide because there is a lack of consensus on the population of Muslims in America. The United States census does not ask for religious affiliation, and as such, many non-Muslim surveys have taken a more conservative estimate, while Muslim organizations have suggested that the population of American Muslims is larger.

[30] http://www.pewforum.org/2011/02/24/religion-in-the-news-Islam-was-no-1-topic-in-2010/. Visited January 1, 2016.

[31] http://www.people-press.org/2014/09/10/growing-concern-about-rise-of-Islamic-extremism-at-home-and-abroad/. Visited January 1, 2016.

[32] Council on American-Islamic Relations, *Legislating Fear: Islamophobia and its Impact on the United States.*

In 2011, the Center for American Progress, a nonpartisan research and educational institute, compiled an extensive report entitled "Fear, Inc." that examined the roots of the Islamophobia network in the United States of America.

According to this report, a "small group of foundations wealthy donors are the lifeblood of the Islamophobia network in America, providing critical funding to a clutch of right-wing think tank that peddle hate and fear of Muslims and Islam – in the form of books, reports, websites, blogs, and carefully crafted talking points that anti-Islam grassroots organizations and some right-wing religious groups use as propaganda for their constituency."[33]

The report indicated that the top seven contributors – whose contributions totaled $42.6 million – to promoting Islamophobia in America, are: Donors Capital Fund, Richard Mellon Scaife Foundations, Lynde and Harry Bradley Foundation, Newton D. & Rochelle F. Becker Foundations and Charitable Trust, Russell Berrie Foundation, Anchorage Charitable Fund and William Rosenwald Family Fund, and Fairbrook Foundation.[34] These major groups provide large amounts of money that support misinformation experts such as: Frank Gaffney, Daniel Pipes, David Yerushalmi, Robert Spencer, and Steven Emerson; and in turn, they spread myths and lies about Islam and Muslims to what is known as the "Islamophobia echo chamber," composed of the religious right, the media, political players, and grassroots organizations.[35] This echo chamber subsequently amplifies fear and misinformation, they mislead the public in adopting anti-Islamic sentiment and activism.

Although each of these groups – that is, the financial contributors, the misinformation experts, religious groups, the media, political players, and grassroots organizations – play major roles in promoting Islamophobia, the two most significant actors who have exacerbated

---

[33] Center for American Progress: *Fear, Inc., The Roots of the Islamophobia Network in America*, p. 2.
[34] Ibid, p. 3.
[35] Ibid, pp. 4-5.

the situation are the media and the political players. In many regards, it is these two who shape public opinion in the United States.

As for the media, various well-developed right-wing outlets provide the Islamophobia network the exposure needed to amplify their message, reach larger audiences, drive fundraising numbers, and grow their membership base. Chief among these media outlets are: the Fox News empire, the National Review magazine and website, *The Washington Times* newspaper and website, the Christian Broadcasting Network and website, and a host of right-wing radio hosts.[36] These media outlets frequently mix coverage of alarmist threats posed by the mere existence of Muslims in America with other news stories and constantly invite well-known Islamophobia misinformation experts to voice and endorse bigoted anti-Islamic views. These media outlets are especially popular among right-wing conservatives and virtually all of the Islamophobia misinformation experts have made recurring appearances on their shows. Unfortunately, the scare tactics employed on these media outlets work.

In a poll conducted by the Public Religion Research Institute, a strong correlation was found between holding erroneous views about Islam and Muslims and watching Fox News.[37] The poll further found that Americans who trust Fox News are the most likely to believe that Muslims have not done enough to oppose extremism, and believe that investigating Muslim extremism is a good idea; nearly twice as many Republicans over Democrats believe that Muslims want to establish Sharīʿa law in America, 31% to 15%; More than 75% of those who mostly trust Fox News believe that Representative Peter King's congressional hearings on Muslim radicalization (that absurdly claimed that 80% of mosques in America were radical!) were a good idea, compared to 45% of those who most trust CNN and 28% of those who most trust public television.[38]

Very frequently, many of these media outlets are quite effectively able to cause national controversy over various issues related to Islam

---

[36] Ibid, p. 85.

[37] Ibid, p. 98.

[38] Ibid.

and Muslims. This is one of the main reasons why many right-wing politicians are so eager to parrot anti-Muslim attacks: because these media outlets allow them to raise funds and get conservative voters to the polls.

The second significant base for amplifying Islamophobia in America is the ability of this network to drench the public with misinformation that is greatly enhanced by elected local and national public officials. These political players essentially push various myths about Islam and Muslims as "facts" and carefully craft political fundraising campaigns and voting strategies based on debunked information.

Among the major Islamophobia political players are the Congress and State House representatives such as: Peter King (R-NY), Sue Myrick (R-NC), Paul Broun (R-GA), Allen West (R-FL), Renee Ellmers (R-NC), Michele Bachmaan (R-MN), John Bennett (R-OK), and many others.

Some of these players, including others such as former Republican Representative and House Speaker Newt Gingrich, even ran for the Presidential elections. These and other elected public officials respond to the fearmongering that occurs through the misinformation experts and media pundits by taking controversial positions on issues such as the role of Sharia, which is constantly painted as being dangerous to America and its values. Anti-Sharia initiatives, in turn, are a way to mobilize anti-Muslim sentiment and increase conservative and right-wing voter turnout.

Interestingly enough, not only is there a rise in Islamophobia in America, but there is also a rise in what may be called "Shiaphobia." Increasingly, many media outlets are portraying various Shīʿa groups in a negative light, suggesting that the Shīʿa are the main cause for much of the sectarian violence and conflict going on in the Middle East and elsewhere. One example is how various militant groups are labeled in media presentations: "Shīʿa rebels" (or more frequently, "Iranian-backed Shīʿa rebels") when referring to the Ḥūthīs in Yemen, or the Iraqi Popular Mobilization Forces (al-Ḥashd al-Shaʿbī); but there is no mention of "Sunnī" al-Qāʿida, Boko Ḥaram, Islamic State, and other groups. Thus, for many Shīʿa residing in the West, there exists the dual challenge of overcoming both Islamophobia and Shiaphobia.

The existence and steady rise of Islamophobia and other forms of anti-Muslim sentiment is creating a serious challenge for Muslim educators and preachers in America. Thus, sustained efforts for suitable daʿwah, both qualitatively and quantitatively, become increasingly more important in the American context.

Chapter Four: Daʿwah and Tablīgh in the West

Daʿwah and tablīgh are quintessential features of every single apostle and messenger sent by God to humankind. God states,

﴿وَلَقَدْ بَعَثْنَا فِي كُلِّ أُمَّةٍ رَّسُولًا أَنِ اعْبُدُوا اللَّهَ وَاجْتَنِبُوا الطَّاغُوتَ﴾

> "And we raised among every people a messenger who enjoined: 'Worship God alone and shun the false deity/deities'."[1]

The journey of divine guidance for humankind began with the initial arrival of Adam on this earth:

﴿قُلْنَا اهْبِطُوا مِنْهَا جَمِيعًا فَإِمَّا يَأْتِيَنَّكُم مِّنِّي هُدًى فَمَن تَبِعَ هُدَايَ
فَلَا خَوْفٌ عَلَيْهِمْ وَلَا هُمْ يَحْزَنُونَ﴾

> "We said: 'Go down from it, all of you. And when guidance comes to you from Me, whoever follows My guidance – there will be no fear concerning them, nor will they grieve'."[2]

The Qur'an further emphasizes that there was never a community that lacked a warner:

﴿وَإِن مِّنْ أُمَّةٍ إِلَّا خَلَا فِيهَا نَذِيرٌ﴾

> "And there was never a nation but that there existed with it a warner."[3]

---

[1] Qur'an, Sūrah al-Naḥl (16), verse 36.
[2] Qur'an, Sūrah al-Baqarah (2), verse 38.
[3] Qur'an, Sūrah al-Fāṭir (35), verse 24.

Imam ʿAlī states: "God chose prophets and took their pledge for His revelation and for carrying His message as their trust."[4] The common denominator among all divine religions and messengers are daʿwah and tablīgh towards monotheism:

﴿وَمَا أَرْسَلْنَا مِنْ قَبْلِكَ مِنْ رَسُولٍ إِلَّا نُوحِي إِلَيْهِ أَنَّهُ لَا إِلَٰهَ إِلَّا أَنَا
فَاعْبُدُونِ﴾

> "And We sent not before you (Muḥammad) any messenger except that We revealed to him that, 'There is no deity except Me, so worship Me'."[5]

Additionally, every messenger also focused on his community's own spatial, temporal, and social contexts when delivering his message. For example, Abraham's primary objective was focused on combating superstitions, polytheism, idol-worship, and subservience to the constellations. This is evident in his own journey of recognizing God, as well as his interactions with his community:

﴿وَكَذَٰلِكَ نُرِي إِبْرَاهِيمَ مَلَكُوتَ السَّمَاوَاتِ وَالْأَرْضِ وَلِيَكُونَ مِنَ
الْمُوقِنِينَ فَلَمَّا جَنَّ عَلَيْهِ اللَّيْلُ رَأَىٰ كَوْكَبًا قَالَ هَٰذَا رَبِّي فَلَمَّا أَفَلَ
قَالَ لَا أُحِبُّ الْآفِلِينَ فَلَمَّا رَأَى الْقَمَرَ بَازِغًا قَالَ هَٰذَا رَبِّي فَلَمَّا أَفَلَ
قَالَ لَئِنْ لَمْ يَهْدِنِي رَبِّي لَأَكُونَنَّ مِنَ الْقَوْمِ الضَّالِّينَ فَلَمَّا رَأَى
الشَّمْسَ بَازِغَةً قَالَ هَٰذَا رَبِّي هَٰذَا أَكْبَرُ فَلَمَّا أَفَلَتْ قَالَ يَا قَوْمِ إِنِّي
بَرِيءٌ مِمَّا تُشْرِكُونَ إِنِّي وَجَّهْتُ وَجْهِيَ لِلَّذِي فَطَرَ السَّمَاوَاتِ وَالْأَرْضَ
حَنِيفًا وَمَا أَنَا مِنَ الْمُشْرِكِينَ وَحَاجَّهُ قَوْمُهُ قَالَ أَتُحَاجُّونِّي فِي اللَّهِ وَقَدْ

---

[4] *Nahj al-Balāghah*, sermon 1.
[5] Qur'an, Sūrah al-Anbiyāʾ (21), verse 25.

هَدَانِ وَلَا أَخَافُ مَا تُشْرِكُونَ بِهِ إِلَّا أَن يَشَاءَ رَبِّي شَيْئًا وَسِعَ رَبِّي كُلَّ
شَيْءٍ عِلْمًا أَفَلَا تَتَذَكَّرُونَ﴾

"And thus did We show Abraham the realm of the heavens and the earth that he would attain certainty [in faith]. So when the night covered him [with darkness], he saw a star. He said, 'This is my lord.' But when it set, he said, 'I like not those that disappear.' And when he saw the moon rising, he said, 'This is my lord.' But when it set, he said, 'Unless my Lord guides me, I will surely be among the people gone astray.' And when he saw the sun rising, he said, 'This is my lord; this is greater.' But when it set, he said, 'O my people, indeed I am free from what you associate with God. Indeed, I have turned my face toward He who created the heavens and the earth, inclining toward truth, and I am not of those who associate others with God.' And his people argued with him. He said, 'Do you argue with me concerning God while He has guided me? And I fear not what you associate with Him [and will not be harmed] unless my Lord should will something. My Lord encompasses all things in knowledge; then will you not remember?'"[6]

Lot's objective focused on combating moral decadence expressed through sexual deviance and promiscuity:

﴿أَتَأْتُونَ الذُّكْرَانَ مِنَ الْعَالَمِينَ وَتَذَرُونَ مَا خَلَقَ لَكُمْ رَبُّكُم مِّنْ
أَزْوَاجِكُم بَلْ أَنتُمْ قَوْمٌ عَادُونَ﴾

"[Lot asked:] 'Do you approach the males and leave what your Lord has created for you as mates? You are a transgressing people.'"[7]

[6] Qur'an, Sūrah al-Anʿām (6), verses 75-81.
[7] Qur'an, Sūrah al-Shuarā' (26), verses 165-166.

Prophet Jethro's focus was on mending corruption within the economic sphere:

﴿وَإِلَىٰ مَدْيَنَ أَخَاهُمْ شُعَيْبًا قَالَ يَا قَوْمِ اعْبُدُوا اللَّهَ مَا لَكُم مِّنْ إِلَٰهٍ غَيْرُهُ وَلَا تَنقُصُوا الْمِكْيَالَ وَالْمِيزَانَ إِنِّي أَرَاكُم بِخَيْرٍ وَإِنِّي أَخَافُ عَلَيْكُمْ عَذَابَ يَوْمٍ مُّحِيطٍ وَيَا قَوْمِ أَوْفُوا الْمِكْيَالَ وَالْمِيزَانَ بِالْقِسْطِ وَلَا تَبْخَسُوا النَّاسَ أَشْيَاءَهُمْ وَلَا تَعْثَوْا فِي الْأَرْضِ مُفْسِدِينَ بَقِيَّتُ اللَّهِ خَيْرٌ لَّكُمْ إِن كُنتُم مُّؤْمِنِينَ وَمَا أَنَا عَلَيْكُم بِحَفِيظٍ﴾

"And to Madyan [We sent] their brother Jethro. He said, 'O my people, worship God; you have no deity other than Him. And do not decrease from the measure and the scale. Indeed, I see you in prosperity, but indeed, I fear for you the punishment of an all-encompassing Day. And O my people, give full measure and weight in justice and do not deprive the people of their due and do not commit abuse on the earth, spreading corruption. What remains [lawful] from God is best for you, if you are believers. But I am not a controller over you.'"[8]

Hūd focused his attention on attaining asceticism and abstinence from worldly extravagance:

﴿أَتَبْنُونَ بِكُلِّ رِيعٍ آيَةً تَعْبَثُونَ وَتَتَّخِذُونَ مَصَانِعَ لَعَلَّكُمْ تَخْلُدُونَ وَإِذَا بَطَشْتُم بَطَشْتُمْ جَبَّارِينَ﴾

"[Hūd asked:] 'Do you construct on every elevation a sign, amusing yourselves? And take for yourselves palaces and

---

[8] Qur'an, Sūrah Hūd (11), verses 84-86.

fortresses that you might abide eternally? And when you strike, you strike as tyrants?'"[9]

Prophet Joseph's attention was focused on good governance:

﴿قَالَ اجْعَلْنِي عَلَىٰ خَزَائِنِ الْأَرْضِ إِنِّي حَفِيظٌ عَلِيمٌ﴾

"He (Joseph) said: 'Appoint me over the storehouses of the land. Indeed, I will be a well acquainted guardian.'"[10]

Prophet David's mission focused on wise judgment:

﴿وَشَدَدْنَا مُلْكَهُ وَآتَيْنَاهُ الْحِكْمَةَ وَفَصْلَ الْخِطَابِ﴾

"And We strengthened his kingdom and gave him wisdom and discernment in speech."[11]

Prophet Moses's objective concerned political and social reforms and combating political arrogance:

﴿نَتْلُو عَلَيْكَ مِن نَّبَإِ مُوسَىٰ وَفِرْعَوْنَ بِالْحَقِّ لِقَوْمٍ يُؤْمِنُونَ إِنَّ فِرْعَوْنَ عَلَا فِي الْأَرْضِ وَجَعَلَ أَهْلَهَا شِيَعًا يَسْتَضْعِفُ طَائِفَةً مِّنْهُمْ يُذَبِّحُ أَبْنَاءَهُمْ وَيَسْتَحْيِي نِسَاءَهُمْ إِنَّهُ كَانَ مِنَ الْمُفْسِدِينَ وَنُرِيدُ أَن نَّمُنَّ عَلَى الَّذِينَ اسْتُضْعِفُوا فِي الْأَرْضِ وَنَجْعَلَهُمْ أَئِمَّةً وَنَجْعَلَهُمُ الْوَارِثِينَ وَنُمَكِّنَ لَهُمْ فِي الْأَرْضِ وَنُرِيَ فِرْعَوْنَ وَهَامَانَ وَجُنُودَهُمَا مِنْهُم مَّا كَانُوا يَحْذَرُونَ﴾

"We recite to you from the news of Prophet Moses and Pharaoh in truth for a people who believe. Indeed, Pharaoh exalted himself in the land and made its people into factions, oppressing a sector among them, slaughtering their

---

[9] Qur'an, Sūrah al-Shuarā' (26), verses 128-130.
[10] Qur'an, Sūrah Yūsuf (12), verse 55.
[11] Qur'an, Sūrah Ṣuad (38), verse 20.

[newborn] sons and keeping their females alive. Surely he was one of the mischief-makers. And We wanted to confer favor upon those who were oppressed in the land, and make them leaders and make them inheritors, and establish them in the land, and show Pharaoh and [his minister] Hāmān[12] and their soldiers through them that which they had feared."[13]

Finally, Prophet Jesus's attention and teaching focused primarily on observing asceticism and adopting sublime ethics:

﴿إِذْ قَالَ اللَّهُ يَا عِيسَى ابْنَ مَرْيَمَ اذْكُرْ نِعْمَتِي عَلَيْكَ وَعَلَىٰ وَالِدَتِكَ
إِذْ أَيَّدْتُكَ بِرُوحِ الْقُدُسِ تُكَلِّمُ النَّاسَ فِي الْمَهْدِ وَكَهْلًا ۖ وَإِذْ عَلَّمْتُكَ
الْكِتَابَ وَالْحِكْمَةَ وَالتَّوْرَاةَ وَالْإِنْجِيلَ ۖ وَإِذْ تَخْلُقُ مِنَ الطِّينِ كَهَيْئَةِ
الطَّيْرِ بِإِذْنِي فَتَنْفُخُ فِيهَا فَتَكُونُ طَيْرًا بِإِذْنِي ۖ وَتُبْرِئُ الْأَكْمَهَ
وَالْأَبْرَصَ بِإِذْنِي ۖ وَإِذْ تُخْرِجُ الْمَوْتَىٰ بِإِذْنِي ۖ وَإِذْ كَفَفْتُ بَنِي إِسْرَائِيلَ
عَنْكَ إِذْ جِئْتَهُمْ بِالْبَيِّنَاتِ فَقَالَ الَّذِينَ كَفَرُوا مِنْهُمْ إِنْ هَٰذَا إِلَّا
سِحْرٌ مُبِينٌ ۝ وَإِذْ أَوْحَيْتُ إِلَى الْحَوَارِيِّينَ أَنْ آمِنُوا بِي وَبِرَسُولِي قَالُوا
آمَنَّا وَاشْهَدْ بِأَنَّنَا مُسْلِمُونَ ۝ إِذْ قَالَ الْحَوَارِيُّونَ يَا عِيسَى ابْنَ مَرْيَمَ
هَلْ يَسْتَطِيعُ رَبُّكَ أَنْ يُنَزِّلَ عَلَيْنَا مَائِدَةً مِنَ السَّمَاءِ ۖ قَالَ اتَّقُوا اللَّهَ
إِنْ كُنْتُمْ مُؤْمِنِينَ ۝ قَالُوا نُرِيدُ أَنْ نَأْكُلَ مِنْهَا وَتَطْمَئِنَّ قُلُوبُنَا
وَنَعْلَمَ أَنْ قَدْ صَدَقْتَنَا وَنَكُونَ عَلَيْهَا مِنَ الشَّاهِدِينَ ۝ قَالَ عِيسَى

---

[12] Hāmān was the minister of the Pharaoh and associated with him in his court at the time of Prophet Moses.

[13] Qur'an, Sūrah al-Qaṣaṣ (28), verses 3-6.

ابْنُ مَرْيَمَ اللَّهُمَّ رَبَّنَا أَنْزِلْ عَلَيْنَا مَايِدَةً مِنَ السَّمَاءِ تَكُونُ لَنَا عِيدًا
لِأَوَّلِنَا وَآخِرِنَا وَآيَةً مِنْكَ ۖ وَارْزُقْنَا وَأَنْتَ خَيْرُ الرَّازِقِينَ ۝ قَالَ اللَّهُ
إِنِّي مُنَزِّلُهَا عَلَيْكُمْ ۖ فَمَنْ يَكْفُرْ بَعْدُ مِنْكُمْ فَإِنِّي أُعَذِّبُهُ عَذَابًا لَا
أُعَذِّبُهُ أَحَدًا مِنَ الْعَالَمِينَ ۝ وَإِذْ قَالَ اللَّهُ يَا عِيسَى ابْنَ مَرْيَمَ أَأَنْتَ
قُلْتَ لِلنَّاسِ اتَّخِذُونِي وَأُمِّيَ إِلَٰهَيْنِ مِنْ دُونِ اللَّهِ ۖ قَالَ سُبْحَانَكَ مَا
يَكُونُ لِي أَنْ أَقُولَ مَا لَيْسَ لِي بِحَقٍّ ۚ إِنْ كُنْتُ قُلْتُهُ فَقَدْ عَلِمْتَهُ ۚ
تَعْلَمُ مَا فِي نَفْسِي وَلَا أَعْلَمُ مَا فِي نَفْسِكَ ۚ إِنَّكَ أَنْتَ عَلَّامُ الْغُيُوبِ
۝ مَا قُلْتُ لَهُمْ إِلَّا مَا أَمَرْتَنِي بِهِ أَنِ اعْبُدُوا اللَّهَ رَبِّي وَرَبَّكُمْ ۚ وَكُنْتُ
عَلَيْهِمْ شَهِيدًا مَا دُمْتُ فِيهِمْ ۖ فَلَمَّا تَوَفَّيْتَنِي كُنْتَ أَنْتَ الرَّقِيبَ
عَلَيْهِمْ ۚ وَأَنْتَ عَلَىٰ كُلِّ شَيْءٍ شَهِيدٌ ۝ إِنْ تُعَذِّبْهُمْ فَإِنَّهُمْ عِبَادُكَ ۖ
وَإِنْ تَغْفِرْ لَهُمْ فَإِنَّكَ أَنْتَ الْعَزِيزُ الْحَكِيمُ ۝ قَالَ اللَّهُ هَٰذَا يَوْمُ يَنْفَعُ
الصَّادِقِينَ صِدْقُهُمْ ۚ لَهُمْ جَنَّاتٌ تَجْرِي مِنْ تَحْتِهَا الْأَنْهَارُ خَالِدِينَ فِيهَا
أَبَدًا ۚ رَضِيَ اللَّهُ عَنْهُمْ وَرَضُوا عَنْهُ ۚ ذَٰلِكَ الْفَوْزُ الْعَظِيمُ﴾

"When God will say, O Jesus son of Mary, remember My blessing upon you and upon your mother, when I strengthened you with the Holy Spirit, so you would speak to the people in the cradle and in adulthood, and when I taught you the Book and wisdom, the Torah and the Evangel, and when you would create from clay the form of a bird, with My leave, and you would breathe into it and it would become a bird, with My leave; and you would heal the blind and the leper, with My leave, and you would raise the dead, with My leave; and when I held off [the evil of] the Children of Israel from you when you brought them manifest proofs, whereat the faithless among them said, 'This is nothing but plain magic.' And when I inspired the Disciples, [saying], 'Have faith in Me and My apostle,' they said, 'We have faith. Bear witness that we are Muslims.' When the Disciples said, 'O Jesus son of Mary! Can your Lord send down to us a table from the sky?' Said he, 'Be wary of God, should you be faithful.' They said, 'We desire to eat from it, and our hearts will be at rest: we shall know that you have told us the truth, and we shall be among the witnesses to it.' Said Jesus son of Mary, 'O God! Our Lord! Send down to us a table from the sky, to be a festival for us, for the first ones and the last ones among us and as a sign from You, and provide for us; for You are the best of providers.' God said, 'I will indeed send it down to you. But should any of you disbelieves after this, I will indeed punish him with a punishment such as I do not punish anyone in all creation.' And when God will say, 'O Jesus son of Mary! Were it you who said to the people, "Take me and my mother for gods besides God"?' He will say, 'Immaculate are You! It does not behoove me to say what I have no right to [say]. Had I said it, You would certainly have known it: You know whatever is in my self, and I do not know what is in Your Self. Indeed You are knower of all that is Unseen. I did not say to them [anything] except what You had commanded me [to say]: "Worship God, my Lord and your Lord." And I was a witness to them so long as I was among them. But when You had taken me away, You Yourself were watchful over them, and You are witness to all things. If You punish them, they are indeed Your creatures; but if You forgive them, You are indeed the All-Mighty, the All-Wise.' God will say, 'This day truthfulness shall benefit the truthful. For them there will be gardens with streams running in them, to remain in them forever. God is pleased with them and they are pleased with Him. That is the great success.'"[14]

Similarly, in the West, Islam and Muslims face a number of challenges that require a specific focus on daʿwah and tablīgh objectives and methods.

The first area of focus lies in the fact that, as a religious minority within a non-Muslim majority (who is largely ignorant about Islam), the main emphasis must be on presenting an accurate understanding of Islam and its worldview.

The second area of attention must be on maintaining an Islamic identity within the ranks of the Muslim community, a segment of which faces the risk of complete absorption into western culture and diversion away from Islam.

The Qurʾan describes the Muslim community as being:

﴿كُنْتُمْ خَيْرَ أُمَّةٍ أُخْرِجَتْ لِلنَّاسِ﴾

"The best community that has been brought forth."[15]

Yet, the standard of superiority or prominence of the Muslims is not open ended or baseless, but rather it is based on the condition of successful daʿwah and tablīgh:

﴿تَأْمُرُونَ بِالْمَعْرُوفِ وَتَنْهَوْنَ عَنِ الْمُنكَرِ وَتُؤْمِنُونَ بِاللَّهِ﴾

"You enjoin what is good and forbid what is evil, and you believe in God."[16]

Furthermore, the very survival and continuity of Islam is based on establishing successful frameworks of daʿwah and tablīgh. In other words, daʿwah and tablīgh ensure the survival of the "life" of Islam and the community of Muslims, as long as they are able to both adopt and propagate this message of "life":

---

[14] Qurʾan, Sūrah al-Māʾidah (5), verses 110-119.
[15] Qurʾan, Sūrah Āle ʿImrān (3), verse 110.
[16] Ibid.

﴿يَا أَيُّهَا الَّذِينَ آمَنُوا اسْتَجِيبُوا لِلَّهِ وَلِلرَّسُولِ إِذَا دَعَاكُمْ لِمَا يُحْيِيكُمْ﴾

> "O believers! Answer the call of God and the Messenger when he calls you to that which gives you life."[17]

Thus, daʿwah and tablīgh are among the most important features of Islam, and a person who holds responsibility for propagating the message of Islam through preaching and education holds a very significant position.

The preacher and educator of Islam and its values is essentially a means by which the message is propagated to the masses. As such, we find that the Islamic traditions describe scholars as heirs to the prophets.[18]

Scholars and preachers employ various tools of communication in order to arrive to their objectives. These may include the presentation of lectures, participation in dialogues and seminars, authoring books, teaching classes, conducting interviews, engaging in multimedia and social media activities, and so on. However, it is essential that Islamic preachers, educators, and scholars realize the significance of approaching this topic within the context of their respective societies, especially in the West.

The Position of Daʿwah in America Today

Over the past few decades, Muslims in America have accomplished many strides in their daʿwah initiatives and activities. However, a great number of challenges continue to exist and there is a long road ahead in advancing and developing Islamic daʿwah in America. Following is a brief survey of the current state and position of daʿwah in the United States.

---

[17] Qurʾan, Sūrah al-Anfāl (8), verse 24.
[18] *Al-Kāfī*, v. 1, p. 134.

Some estimates place the current number of Islamic centers, mosques, and organizations in America at over 2,100.[19] However, a large number of these centers and mosques seem to mostly cater to the Muslim immigrant communities, which make up the majority of the Muslim population in America. Many of these centers are highly ethnocentric, and focus their programs and methods specifically to their own nationalities, ethnicities, and communities. As mentioned earlier, various centers hold their ongoing programs in their native Arabic, Persian, Urdu, and other non-English languages.

Despite the slow increase in the number of American-born imams and resident scholars at various mosques and centers, the vast majority of these leaders continue to be immigrants who unfortunately do not possess adequate English language skills. In fact, during the course of various interviews that I conducted with both Sunnī and Shīʿa scholars, educators, and leaders situated across the country, virtually all of the interviewees stated that one of the biggest challenges to daʿwah in America was the severe lack of English-speaking preachers. Some of the preachers who do speak English tend to have a strong native accent, making their English language very difficult to understand.

Islamic centers and mosques are often not adequately equipped for Islamic daʿwah activities, contrary to Christian and other religious organizations and churches. Most Islamic centers do not publish English language materials, if any publications at all; and this is especially the case with Shīʿa mosques and centers. For example, when I was writing my book introductory book *Discovering Islam* over a decade ago, I found that the number of suitable introductory books to Islam authored by Shīʿa writers in America were less than ten, while Sunnī authors had compiled such materials in the hundreds. Not only is there a gap in the number of suitable resources for daʿwah, but many mosques do not even possess the limited number of resources available for reference and distribution.

---

[19] http://usatoday30.usatoday.com/news/religion/story/2012-02-29/Islamic-worship-growth-us/53298792/1. Visited January 1, 2016.

Nonetheless, a small minority of American Islamic centers focus their attention on daʿwah concerns and thus, widen their emphasis to include the convert and non-Muslim communities.

It may be observed that Sunnī organizations are much more effective in daʿwah initiatives and activities and in turn, are able to attract a higher number of converts to Islam than Shīʿa organizations. This is the case because, not only do Sunnī organizations far outnumber Shīʿa organizations in quantity, but also excel in both financial and human resources.

Furthermore, Sunnī organizations are more focused, prepared, and organized for daʿwah initiatives. Many are well-equipped with daʿwah materials and they conduct their programs entirely in the English language. Additionally, some of these centers have specific programs that are conducted solely for the purpose of attracting non-Muslims to their centers and to Islam. Not only do these centers invite to Islam, but also maintain programs in order to keep converts engaged and part of the community.

The vast majority of Shīʿa centers and mosques on the contrary, seem to be ritual-focused. They seldom focus on the issue of daʿwah. Thus, it may be suggested that, save the very rare cases, daʿwah is non-existent in Shīʿa organizations. This raises a red flag. Some centers are decades old, yet have not attracted a single convert to Islam. An important reason for this is that a large portion of the Shīʿa communities in the West misunderstands their goals and objectives.

Theoretical and Practical Daʿwah

There are two aspects to daʿwah: the theoretical and the practical. The theoretical aspect of daʿwah entails an academic study of the theories and methods related to it; however, the practical aspect includes field-work and immersion in daʿwah activities. Similar to other fields, there is a great deal of difference between the two. It is only when a preacher specifically enters into the field and applies daʿwah initiatives that he/she realizes a completely different dimension to daʿwah - one that is fruitful and productive.

Many preachers are shocked when they enter into the field of practical daʿwah, because although they may have been educated regarding theoretical daʿwah, they do not possess the experience to be completely successful in the practical sphere. Thus, it may be encouraged that a preacher begins his/her journey as an associate imam or preacher, so that he/she is able to gain some insight into practical daʿwah activities and such related issues.

Potentials of Daʿwah

The potentials of daʿwah in America cannot be compared to anywhere else in the world, including the European countries. This is due to a number of significant reasons.

Firstly, the United States prides itself on the constitutional right of freedom of religion. Virtually every religious creed or group can freely practice, preach, and promote their own messages, without facing any governmental or political restrictions or hindrances. This right is inalienable and guaranteed for all citizens by the First Amendment to the Constitution of the United States. This foundation of religious freedom has allowed religious diversity to flourish in America.

According to Diana Eck, the principles of "nonestablishment" of religion and the "free exercise" of religion "have provided a sturdy rudder through the past two centuries as [America's] religious diversity has expanded. After all, religious freedom is the fountainhead of religious diversity. The two go inextricably together."[20]

Of course, the history of the United States reminds us that widespread religious freedom was a hard won battle in this land. The historic controversies over religious freedom, tolerance, and differences sometimes ended in imprisonment, torture, and even death.

Interestingly, the heated arguments that ensued as early as the seventeenth century in America were not between Christians and secularists, but rather they were intensely religious whereby both establishment of religion and toleration of religious differences were articulated in theological terms. At any rate, the past few centuries of

---

[20] *A New Religious America*, p. 7.

American history witnessed a long and difficult battle that resulted in the protection of religious freedom that were enshrined in the Bill of Rights in 1791.

It must be noted however, that the existence of religious freedom and diversity does not automatically translate into a nation free of religious discrimination and prejudice. As mentioned in the section on Islamophobia, anti-Muslim sentiment and vilification is still present in the United States, and continues to be one of the greatest challenges of religious freedom for Muslims in America.

Nonetheless, adding to religious freedom and diversity, religious organizations are encouraged to be productive and expand their work. For example, religious organizations that file for and are legally recognized as non-profit are also able to acquire federal tax-exempt status. This designation allows exemption from federal corporate and income taxes for most types of revenue. Also, organizations designated as tax-exempt are able to solicit tax deductible contributions. In fact, in some cases, these organizations may be able to receive governmental funding. One example of this is what is known as the White House Office of Faith-based and Neighborhood Partnerships. One of their goals is to make sure that neighborhood organizations are aware of relevant grant opportunities from the Federal Government.[21]

The second major reason that adds to the great potential for daʿwah initiatives in America is that the means of religious propagation are readily available and easily accessible. For example, the Internet is one of the most important and popular means of religious propagation.

According to the U.S. Census Bureau, in 2013, 83.8% of U.S. households reported computer ownership, with 78.5% of all households having a desktop or laptop computer, and 63.6% having a handheld computer. Furthermore, 74.4% of all households reported Internet use, with 73.4% reporting a high speed connection.[22]

---

[21] More information about this initiative may be found here: https://www.whitehouse.gov/administration/eop/ofbnp/about. Visited January 1, 2016.

[22] http://www.census.gov/hhes/computer/. Visited January 1, 2016.

Such a high rate of access to the Internet means that more people are able to both propagate religious teachings, as well as have easier access to them. This may be achieved through websites, blogs, social media, videos, and other means. However, it must be noted that the Internet has been a tool for both positive and destructive religious propagation.

Unfortunately, not only are positive messages about Islam being presented through the Internet, but negative and destructive views and perceptions are also being transmitted. For example, according to a report by the Brookings Institution, in the fall of 2014, there were approximately 46,000 Twitter users actively supporting the so-called "Islamic State"; and 400 of those users claimed on their profiles that they lived in the United States.[23]

Of course, the Internet is but one medium for religious dissemination. Other examples include the abundance of other media sources, such as television and radio stations and shows, as well as written materials and publications. Muslim organizations, centers, activists, scholars, and leaders have adopted many of these mediums in their daʿwah activities in the United States.

Other potential avenues for daʿwah in the United States consist of: holding various camps and retreats; establishment of office of daʿwah and outreach at mosques and Islamic centers; annual conventions and conferences (such as those held by national organizations such as the Muslim Group of USA and Canada, the Universal Muslim Association of America (UMAA), the Islamic Society of North America (ISNA), the Islamic Circle of North America (ICNA), the Muslim Student Association (MSA), the Council on American-Islamic Relations (CAIR), the Muslim Public Affairs Council (MPAC), and others); on college and university campuses (such as information booths, seminars, etc.); at religious organizations and events (churches, synagogues, temples, etc.); at think-tank organizations (such as the Council on Foreign Relations, etc.); in the military, prisons, and hospitals through

---

[23] http://www.brookings.edu/~/media/research/files/papers/2015/03/isis-twitter-census-berger-morgan/isis_twitter_census_berger_morgan.pdf. Visited January 1, 2016.

chaplaincy; and through social/community service projects (such as relief organizations, free medical clinics, soup kitchens, homeless shelters, charities, walks, etc.).

Approaches of Daʿwah and Tablīgh

In the age of advanced technology and mass communication, there is a wide array of tools and approaches to be employed in areas of daʿwah and tablīgh. One of these approaches is through oral communication such as through lectures, seminars, conferences, workshops, classes, homilies, debates and discussions, television and radio interviews, Friday sermons, and the Ḥusaynī sessions (majālis).

A second approach is through the composition of literature through books, op-eds, magazines, blogs, essays, periodicals, and social media posts (Facebook, Twitter, etc.).

A third avenue is through artistic representation: poetry, paintings, calligraphy, artifacts, galleries, audio/video programming, plays, and movies.

A fourth approach is through youth and family camps and retreats. Finally, a fifth approach is through trips to historic and religious sites, such as *ʿumra*, *ḥajj*, and various places of *ziyārāt.*

In addition to these and other approaches to daʿwah and tablīgh, it is also important for the educator, preacher, writer, or scholar to engage in a specific manner with these approaches.

One of the most important manners for preachers is that preaching should be compatible with the spatial and temporal demands and contexts. Topics, discussions, and styles of preaching must be contemporary and relevant. The focus of discussions and presentations should not be on abstracts that are completely disconnected from society's needs. This is because society is in need of relevant and practical issues. It is the educator's duty therefore, to pinpoint the pressing needs and problems of his/her constituency and then address them head-on.

Secondly, it is imperative that the preacher maintains moderation and equilibrium in addressing the various issues of the community. In other words, the preacher should never take a one-sided approach to issues, but rather must focus on a collective and wholesome understanding. For example, some preachers focus their attention only on combating the issue of polytheism through the worship/visitation of graves while neglecting other vital concerns. On the other hand, some preachers focus only on the issue of Ḥusaynī shaʿāyer (rituals) and neglect important moral and social issues. Other preachers focus only on political issues, neglecting spiritual issues. A more effective approach to preaching is to be wholesome and complete in our discussions and education.

Thirdly, every preacher living in the United States, and the West more generally, must focus on the issue of inclusivity and exclusivity. Muslims in the West live in religiously and culturally pluralistic societies, therefore, it is imperative for Muslims to understand that to live in diverse and pluralistic societies entails moving beyond 'tolerance of' to 'embracing others'. Preachers must avoid derogatory, hateful, and condescending speech and tones towards various religious traditions or schools of thought. They must also avoid the issue of excommunication, from bother other schools of thought and other religions. This has become a prevalent phenomenon in many circles, and one that is very dangerous. We are reminded that the Holy Qurʾan emphasizes wisdom and good admonishment when preaching the way or path to God.[24]

A fourth approach to preaching is that it the preacher should be non-partisan, because his/her prime objective is to guide people to God. Thus, the preacher works for God, not a specific group, party, or faction; and consequently, the preacher must be open to dialogue, not diatribe. Partisanship essentially leads to narrow-mindedness, because one considers his/her own group and ideas as being superior to others. Partisanship also entails preference for one's own self-interests over others. The preacher's objective must be broader and more inclusive. There is a correlation between sincerity to God and openness to others. This includes avoiding repression, and acceptance to opposite opinions. The Qurʾan illustrates the manner of Prophet Muḥammad:

---

[24] Qurʾan, Sūrah al-Naḥl (16), verse 125.

"Either we or you are rightly guided or in manifest error."[25] The Prophet's message was based on dialogue.

Content of Daʿwah and Tablīgh

As mentioned previously, successful preaching is based on two principles: the moral, intellectual, and practical characteristics of the preacher, as well as the content of the preacher's message. If the content of the message is not appropriate or correct, then the results of preaching will be counter-productive. Instead of guidance, there will be misleading; instead of bringing people's hearts and minds towards adopting religion and faith, there will be rejection of religion and faith.

We must remember that the content and message of preaching in the context of the West differs greatly from that in other parts of the world, especially the Middle East. This is because firstly, Muslims are a minority in the West; and secondly, there is a rapid rise of Islamophobia among westerners due to the increase of religious violent extremism in parts of the Muslim world.

Content of Daʿwah

The content of daʿwah activities, that is those related to preaching Islam to non-Muslims may be categorized into four areas. The first of these concerns philosophical, theological, and ideological issues. Special attention should be paid to the following concepts:

a. **Monotheism** (*tawḥīd*). It is clear that monotheism serves as the foundational theological basis of Islam. It is imperative that preachers are able to clearly and thoroughly present the Islamic perspective of monotheism, and how the Islamic view compares and contrasts to other religious views. Added to this is also the preacher's ability to counter various contemporary atheistic arguments that have become prevalent and popular today.

b. **Hereafter** (*maʿād*). In the Islamic tradition, the concept of the Hereafter is closely associated to the concept of belief in God and

[25] Qur'an, Sūrah al-Saba (34), verse 24.

monotheism. The former represents the origin, while the latter represents the destination, and according to the Qur'an, both are one: "To God we belong and to Him we will return."[26] It is essential that preachers are able to adequately educate and relate the Islamic understanding of the Hereafter to non-Muslims, including the differences between religious traditions regarding heaven and hell, self and group accountability, and divine justice.

c. **Prophethood** (*nubuwwah*). The concept and place of prophets and messengers varies from religion to religion. It is essential that a preacher is able to relate the similarities and differences between the status and role of prophets and messengers according to the Islamic tradition and other religious traditions. A special area of focus may be the comparison between prophets Jesus and Muḥammad.

d. **Qur'an and Bible**. Similar to the concept of prophethood, the status and role of scripture in Islamic tradition varies in many respects to that of other religious traditions. Often, non-Muslims assume that the Qur'an's status is equal to that of the Bible, while misunderstanding the significant differences between these texts. Furthermore, it is essential to point out that not only do Muslims consider the Qur'an to be the verbatim Word of God, but that the Qur'an is free from all types of alteration as well. In fact, the issue of alteration and corruption of the Qur'an is one that is highly misunderstood even within the Islamic tradition among various schools of thought and therefore must be addressed accordingly.

e. **Islam as the final divine message**. Various studies, reports, and surveys suggest that many Americans consider Islam to have little or nothing to do with their own religious traditions. Islam is often seen as a foreign religion, sometimes a "cult." It is essential that preachers make it clear that Islam is a continuation of the divine message that included Judaism and Christianity, and that it is the final one of these divine religions.

---

[26] Qur'an, Sūrah al-Baqarah (2), verse 156.

f. **Other issues**, such as the belief in divine mercy (as related to monotheism), succession to the prophet, and similar theological and ideological concepts.

The second area of focus in daʿwah content pertains to current and contemporary issues. Topics that fall into this category include: religious freedom, pluralism, tolerance, blasphemy, apostasy; religious extremism and violence; human rights, freedom of expression, and the sanctity of human life; the Islamic penal code and sharīʿah. These and other similar contemporary topics form the focus of the various debates about Islam, both within Muslim circles and outside of them. Frequently, these topics are the first to be raised in discussion with non-Muslims about Islam. It is imperative that preachers have a solid grasp on these issues, and moreover they are able to portray them to various audiences in an appropriate manner.

The third category within the scope of daʿwah comprises of various social issues, such as: marriage and family life; gender related issues and the role and status of women in Islam; the meaning and purpose of ḥijāb; honor killings and polygamy. Similar to other contemporary issues, the status and role of women also takes up one of the most prominent spots in current discussions about Islam. Frequently, those who espouse anti-Islamic views attempt to portray the religion as one that is demeaning and oppressive to women.

Finally, the fourth category concerning daʿwah content pertains to ethical and moral issues, such as: compassion, love, mercy, forgiveness, and ethical interactions. We know from examining of the lives of the prophets, messengers, and Ahlulbayt that ethical and moral attitudes serve as the basis for genuine and effective daʿwah activities.

Content of Tablīgh

As for the content related to tablīgh, which entails preaching Islamic teachings to the Muslims themselves, there is a wide array of subjects that are essential to be focused on.

First of all, the role of Islam and Muslims in the West. It is essential for Muslims in America and in the West to understand that their role is not confined to individual religious observances, but that each and every Muslim is an ambassador for their faith in their respective community. Thus, preachers should emphasize the very significant role that Muslims must play both in their own lives as well as in their respective communities. The role of educating others about Islam is not confined to a preacher or a scholar. Each and every Muslim is able to represent Islam accordingly, through their conduct and interactions with friends, classmates, colleagues, and strangers.

Second, preachers must emphasize the significance citizenship and integration into the American society. As mentioned in previous sections, Muslims in America, especially immigrants, tend to fall into various categories: some isolate themselves from American society, while others completely assimilate into society. The negative consequences of both of these trends was also highlighted. Instead, Muslims must understand the vital role of integrating suitably into the American society. According to Imam ʿAlī, "The best country is that which embraces you, not the one that burdens you."[27] This includes love of one's country and observing one's responsibility towards building one's nation.

Unfortunately, many American Muslim immigrants continue to express what some have called "the myth of return": a strong sense of nostalgia and desire to one day return to their homelands and countries of origin.[28] Consequently, many continue to mitigate their engagements in the necessary cultural, political, and civic adjustments of their communities. They feel no sense of belonging in the United States, and consider this country to be a temporary place of residence in preparation for their return.

It is essential to remember that although many of these immigrants may continue to harbor a strong desire to return to their homelands, their children who are born and raised in the United States do not necessarily hold these same sentiments. In fact, in the United States, there currently exists more than one generation of Muslims who consider themselves purely American, with no connection to "The

---

27 *Nahj al-Balāghah*, maxim 442.
28 *Shi'ism in America*, p. 25.

East" whatsoever. Thus, it is vital for the American Muslim community to understand its significant role within the American society. It must move beyond this myth of return and embrace its new homeland; and it must cooperate with other communities in the process of building and maintaining this nation. Each and every Muslim must remember his/her promise to be loyal and committed to the nation, its constitution, and its laws.

Strongly related to the concept of integration and citizenship is the emphasis and focus on the United States foreign policy among many American Muslims. Most American Muslims are very aware of what is happening in other parts of the world, especially in Muslim majority countries. Although this is very important, frequently this focus comes at the expense of a wholesome and broader understanding of American policies, especially those that center on domestic issues. For example, many American Muslims are registered voters, and participate in the presidential elections. However, it is safe to say that a large number of American Muslims are not so enthusiastic about participation in state and local elections. Many do not know their state or local representatives and do not engage with them at all. This is problematic because it is these very representatives that are highly influential when it comes to domestic policies and issues.

It may be noteworthy to mention here that there are some who argue against political and civic engagement in non-Muslim societies, and in fact proceed further in their arguments in expressions of hostility by referring to the concepts of *dār al-ḥarb* and *dār al-Islam*. Essentially, this argument suggests that the world is divided into two abodes: territories belonging to the Muslims (*dār al-Islam*), and those belonging to non-Muslims (*dār al-ḥarb*). This dichotomous division of the world stems from the presumed permanent state of war between Muslims and non-Muslims that was a function of the formative years of Islam, from approximately the eighth to tenth centuries. Accepting the context of hostility between nations as a given, many Muslim jurists considered Muslims to be in a perpetual state of self-defense. Consequently, the Muslim empire frequently found itself in a state of war with other nations and empires. However, this dichotomous view of the two abodes was not the only dominant perspective at the time.

Other jurists added a third category to the division, known as the abode of non-belligerence or neutrality (*dār al-ṣulḥ* or *al-ʿahd*). According to this view, the third abode referred to one that was not Muslim, but that had a peaceful relationship with the Muslim world. This peaceful relationship would usually be based on the payment of a poll tax (*jizyah*) on part of the non-Muslim state. Consequently, it was impermissible to engage in hostility with such an abode.

Although these views were prevalent during their times, it must be stated that they were a function of their historical contexts. Writing on topics of what is now known as international law, Muslim jurists incorporated the practices of their day and age in the interpretation of the Qurʾan and Prophetic Tradition.

Similarly, it is important for contemporary discussions on Muslim and non-Muslim relations to also take into consideration our current contexts. Thus, we find that as Muslim history progressed, the dichotomous and tripartite categorizations of the world became increasingly unrealistic. This is why we find that some jurists and scholars have argued for further classifications of the world, such as that of the abode of justice (*dār al-ʿadl*). Under this category, any nation or territory that exercises justice or allows Muslims to freely and openly practice their religion, will be one that is considered a part of the Muslim world, and relations will be deemed positive and peaceful.[29] Thus, not only would violence and fighting be prohibited in such territories, but Muslims would be mandated to fully participate, integrate in, and care for the building of such abodes. We find that the Qurʾan in fact commands the implementation of justice and benevolence in such cases:

﴿أَن تَبَرُّوهُمْ وَتُقْسِطُوا إِلَيْهِمْ﴾

[29] Abou El Fadl, Khaled, *The Great Theft*, p. 228.

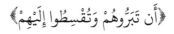

"...from being righteous towards them and acting justly towards them." [30]

Third, preachers must emphasize and focus on various ethical and moral issues. American Muslims face a number of formidable challenges in their daily lives. These include issues related to family cohesion, parenting, safeguarding of family and children, marriage and spousal selection, inter-gender relations, challenges facing the youth, business/financial transactions, and many others. One of the most important features of a successful preacher in the West is his/her ability to guide the community concerning their daily struggles as American Muslims yearn for practical solutions to their various ongoing challenges.

Organizations and Foundations of Daʿwah and Tablīgh

As mentioned above, there are numerous ways in which American Muslims have engaged in daʿwah and tablīgh activities across the country. However, a closer examination reveals that there are currently a number of organizations and foundations that have been established for specific daʿwah initiatives. Some of these organizations are local, while others are national, and some are even international.

Across the United States, local Islamic centers and mosques have been established in virtually every state and major city. In fact, some regions boast dozens of Islamic centers. For example, in southern California, there are over 60 Islamic organizations. Some of the local centers across the United States have been established specifically for daʿwah purposes; these include: the Islamic Daʿwah Center (Houston, Texas),[31] al-Ajwah Islamic Daʿwah Learning Center (San Francisco,

---

[30] Qur'an, Sūrah al-Mumtahanah (60), verse 8.
[31] http://www.islamicdawahcenter.org/. Visited January 1, 2016.

California),[32]),[33] Daʿwah Center of America (Atlanta, Georgia),[34] Islamic Daʿwah Center (Milwaukee, Wisconsin),[35] among others.

In addition to local organizations, there are a number of regional and national Islamic daʿwah organizations; which include: the Latino American Daʿwah Organization (LADO),[36] Muslim Ummah of North America (UMNA), Ministry of W. Deen Mohammed,[37] and others.

Finally the third component of daʿwah and tablīgh in the West include various activists, entrepreneurs, and freelance scholars and preachers. They mostly spend individual and isolated efforts.

Characteristics of Educators and Preachers

There are two significant foundations to successful preaching of Islam, whether in the form of daʿwah or tablīgh. The first is the content and message, and the second is the character and attributes of the educator and preacher. Although the content of the message is absolutely vital, of equal importance, if not more, relate to the characteristics of the preacher him/herself. This is because the main objective of preaching is to guide people to the straight path of God, and as such, the preacher's character must be compatible with his/her enormous task. The Qurʾan describes the preacher as a reviver:

﴿وَمَنْ أَحْيَاهَا فَكَأَنَّمَا أَحْيَا النَّاسَ جَمِيعًا﴾

> "And whoever saves a human life shall be regarded as having saved all mankind."[38]

According to various narrations, the revival of human beings entails their spiritual, moral, and intellectual enhancement. Thus, there are three dimensions of focus pertaining to the characteristics of a preacher in America: the moral, the intellectual, and the practical.

---

[32] http://www.islamicdawahcenter.org/. Visited January 1, 2016.
[33] http://al-ajwah.org/. Visited January 1, 2016.
[34] http://www.dawahcenterus.org/. Visited January 1, 2016.
[35] http://www.dawahcenter.org/. Visited January 1, 2016.
[36] http://www.latinodawah.org. Visited January 1, 2016.
[37] http://www.uscmo.org/members/. Visited January 1, 2016.
[38] Qurʾan, Sūrah al-Māʾidah (5), verse 32.

Moral Characteristics

The moral characteristics of a preacher or educator are: First, to refine and nurture oneself before reaching out to educate and inspire others. The Qur'an asserts this notion:

﴿وَمَنْ أَحْسَنُ قَوْلًا مِّمَّن دَعَا إِلَى اللَّهِ وَعَمِلَ صَالِحًا وَقَالَ إِنَّنِي مِنَ الْمُسْلِمِينَ﴾

> "Who is better in speech than one who invites people to God, and (who) works righteousness, and says: 'I am of those who submit (to Islam).'"[39]

Imam ʿAlī says: "Whoever appoints himself as a leader for the people should begin teaching himself before teaching others and let him nurture people with his behavior before his speech; for the one who refines and teaches himself is more deserving of respect than the one who teaches and refines people."[40]

From my personal experience, I have seen that effective and transformative educators are those who have first achieved self-transformation.

Second, the preacher must be whole heartedly absorbed and dedicated to one's subject, idea, or objective. Sometimes, it may be that the preacher believes in the authenticity and validity of certain concepts, but does not adopt them ones self. On the other hand, sometimes, a preacher adopts the principles, but does not enthusiastically believe in them. Many classical preachers, especially in the sphere of morals, consider preaching as a means of personal income and provision, not a means to positively transform people. This is evident when they do not implement the very teachings that they are preaching themselves. The Qur'an states:

﴿وَجَحَدُوا بِهَا وَاسْتَيْقَنَتْهَا أَنفُسُهُمْ ظُلْمًا وَعُلُوًّا﴾

---

[39] Qur'an, Sūrah al-Fuṣṣilāt (41), verse 33.
[40] *Nahj al-Balāghah*, maxim 73.

> "And they rejected them (the signs of God) in inequity and arrogance, though their hearts were convinced of them."[41]

It is unfortunate that some people are governed by personal advantages, not principles.

Third, a preacher must adopt earnestness and absolute dedication to God in one's life and line of work. Imam ʿAlī states: "When a preacher dedicates one's self to God, then God will chooses him."[42]

Sincerity (*ikhlāṣ*) is the precondition to the acceptance of deeds and it is the essence of faith, and as such, it must be the ultimate motive of a preacher.

The Prophet said: "Dedicate your heart [to God], and your little actions will be sufficient for you."[43] In some cases, preachers work for certain governmental or political entities, or they attempt to appease the organizers or founders of Islamic centers, and as such they derail the lofty objectives of preaching. Furthermore, a preacher must possess absolute trust in God (*tawakkul*). God states:

﴿وَمَن يَتَوَكَّلْ عَلَى اللَّهِ فَهُوَ حَسْبُهُ﴾

> "And whoever puts one's trust in God, He will suffice him."[44]

Very often, daʿwah and tablīgh are tumultuous and surrounded by difficulties. A preacher must have strong support in order to overcome the difficulties of preaching. Some preachers rest their hopes on their audiences and followers as support and backing, but when difficulties events arise, the community may fail them. This is why absolute trust in God is necessary, for the support of God is unmatched.

Nevertheless, it is important to note that *tawakkul* does not mean the cessation of means, but rather it implies that one does not entirely depend on the means while neglecting the ultimate role of God. This indicates that a preacher must express absolute delegation of one's affairs to God. Imam Ḥusayn, under the most severe circumstances, did

---

[41] Qurʾan, Sūrah al-Naml (27), verse 14.
[42] *Nahj al-Balāghah*, maxim 252.
[43] *Biḥār al-Anwār*, v. 70, p. 175.
[44] Qurʾan, Sūrah al-Ṭalāq (65), verse 3.

not forget to renew his allegiance and devotion to God, when he said: "My Lord, You are my trust in every affliction, my hope in every severity, and You are in everything that afflicts or befalls me a trust and tool." [45]

The fourth moral characteristic is that a preacher must possess perseverance. Working for Islam is surrounded with various impediments and requires a great deal of perseverance. Thus, God reminds His Prophet:

﴿فَاصْبِرْ كَمَا صَبَرَ أُولُو الْعَزْمِ مِنَ الرُّسُلِ﴾

"Therefore patiently persevere, as did all of the messengers of firm resolve."[46]

﴿وَاصْبِرْ نَفْسَكَ مَعَ الَّذِينَ يَدْعُونَ رَبَّهُم بِالْغَدَاةِ وَالْعَشِيِّ يُرِيدُونَ وَجْهَهُ﴾

"And keep your soul content with those who call on their lord morning and evening, seeking His pleasure."[47]

﴿وَاصْبِرْ عَلَىٰ مَا يَقُولُونَ وَاهْجُرْهُمْ هَجْرًا جَمِيلًا﴾

"And have patience with what they say, and leave them with noble dignity"[48]

And:

﴿فَاسْتَقِمْ كَمَا أُمِرْتَ﴾

"Therefore stand firm on the straight path as you have been commanded."[49]

---

45 Al-Māzandarānī, Muḥammad Ṣāliḥ, *Sharḥ Uṣūl al-Kāfī*, v. 1, p. 454.
46 Qur'an, Sūrah al-Aḥqāf (46), verse 35.
47 Qur'an, Sūrah al-Kahf (18), verse 28.
48 Qur'an, Sūrah al-Muzzammil (73), verse 10.
49 Qur'an, Sūrah Hūd (11), verse 112.

Often, a preacher or educator may face harassment from the people or other difficulties in various situations. It is essential that a preacher is able to exhibit perseverance and patience when facing such trials.

The fifth characteristic is honesty which serves as the foundation of all human interactions. History shows us that one of the two main epithets that our Holy Prophet had acquired even before the inception of his prophetic mission was honesty. The Qur'an introduces honesty to be one of the key bases of success:

﴿يَا أَيُّهَا الَّذِينَ آمَنُوا اتَّقُوا اللَّهَ وَكُونُوا مَعَ الصَّادِقِينَ﴾

> "O believers, be conscious of God and be with those who are true (in word and deed)."[50]

People's natural disposition is to follow and be inspired by those who speak the truth. In the context of educating and preaching, speaking the truth entails being extra cautious and accurate in both speech and the relation of issues, events, and sources.

The sixth moral characteristic is to exhibit genuine care and compassion to one's audience through humility. One of the primary examples of this sort of care and humility found within our tradition is exemplified by Prophet Jesus who used to wish his followers' feet. Furthermore, the Qur'an tells us that Prophet Muḥammad was:

﴿حَرِيصٌ عَلَيْكُم بِالْمُؤْمِنِينَ رَءُوفٌ رَّحِيمٌ﴾

> "Extremely concerned for you, merciful and most kind to the believers."[51]

Humility, care, and compassion go a long way in effectively inspiring and teaching people.

Seventh, preachers must avoid extravagance in their appearance and demeanor. For example, some preachers insist on adopting a lavish lifestyle by only wearing designer clothing or traveling in luxury. The Qur'an reminds us:

---

[50] Qur'an, Sūrah al-Tawbah (9), verse 119.
[51] Ibid., verse 128.

﴿وَلَا تَمُدَّنَّ عَيْنَيْكَ إِلَىٰ مَا مَتَّعْنَا بِهِ أَزْوَاجًا مِّنْهُمْ زَهْرَةَ الْحَيَاةِ الدُّنْيَا لِنَفْتِنَهُمْ فِيهِ وَرِزْقُ رَبِّكَ خَيْرٌ وَأَبْقَىٰ﴾

"And do not strain your eyes in longing for the things that We have given for enjoyment to parties of them, the splendor of the life of this world, through which We test them, but the provision of your Lord is better and more enduring."[52]

It is observed that some preachers begin their journeys with the intention of preaching, but transform it into merchants later. As a result, their work became futile.

Eighth, preachers must attempt to avoid feeling despondent or frustrated with the lack of apparent transformation. It may be quite depressing for educators to put time, effort, and sincerity in their work to transform people and communities for the better, but they see a lack of or very slow progress in transformation. Educators must constantly remind themselves that guidance and transformation is in the hands of God. The Qur'an states:

﴿لَّيْسَ عَلَيْكَ هُدَاهُمْ وَلَٰكِنَّ اللَّهَ يَهْدِي مَن يَشَاءُ﴾

"It is not upon you (O Messenger) to guide them, but God sets on the right path whom He pleases"[53]

﴿إِنَّكَ لَا تَهْدِي مَنْ أَحْبَبْتَ وَلَٰكِنَّ اللَّهَ يَهْدِي مَن يَشَاءُ﴾

"Surely you will not be able to guide everyone whom you love, rather, it is God who guides whom He wills"[54]

And:

﴿أَفَأَنتَ تُكْرِهُ النَّاسَ حَتَّىٰ يَكُونُوا مُؤْمِنِينَ﴾

---

[52] Qur'an, Sūrah Ṭahā (20), verse 131.
[53] Qur'an, Sūrah al-Baqarah (2), verse 272.
[54] Qur'an, Sūrah al-Qaṣaṣ (28), verse 56.

"Will you then force people until they become believers?"[55]

Ninth, it is imperative that preachers and educators adopt unwavering determination and firmness in confronting corruption, deviation, twisted ideology, radicalism, extremism, innovations, and social ills. The preacher's guide should be the Qur'an:

﴿الَّذِينَ يُبَلِّغُونَ رِسَالَاتِ اللَّهِ وَيَخْشَوْنَهُ وَلَا يَخْشَوْنَ أَحَدًا إِلَّا اللَّهَ﴾

"Those who preach the message of God and fear Him [alone] and who do not fear anyone besides God."[56]

This characteristic is especially significant because it may be observed that some segments of society tend to expect the preacher to compromise certain Islamic principles and values in order to suit their own narrow interests. As an example, in some Islamic centers and mosques, preachers are frequently approached by a member of the board or community, asking them not to mention or emphasize the concepts of *ḥijāb* or *khums*. This may be because that specific individual does not believe in or practice these or other values, and as such expect the preacher to avoid discussing these topics as well.

However a preacher must be resolute in adopting principles and not succumb to these demands, because to do so would be to compromise the role of a genuine preacher. In the tradition of our Prophet, we find a fine example in this regard when the Quraysh demanded him to relinquish his message, but he answered: "By God, if I have possession of the sun in my right hand and the moon in my left, in order to relinquish this message I will not do so until God makes me victorious, or I perish in this path."[57]

Finally, successful preachers require magnanimity of character, tolerance, and forbearance. A preacher must not easily be provoked and this is because in one's work, a preacher will encounter all sorts of people, including those who are very critical, negative, and

---

[55] Qur'an, Sūrah Yūnus (10), verse 99.
[56] Qur'an, Sūrah al-Aḥzāb (33), verse 39.
[57] Al-Ḥalabī, *Al-Sīrah al-Ḥalabiyyah*, v. 1, p. 462.

condescending. The preacher must not react in a negative way to provocations, and must choose one's words carefully when speaking and employ broadmindedness. Sometimes, when a person is reminded of mishaps and mistakes, one must be accepting of them. The Qur'an relays to us Prophet Moses's request from God when he was charged with addressing Pharaoh:

﴿قَالَ رَبِّ اشْرَحْ لِي صَدْرِي﴾

> "[Prophet Moses] said: O my Lord, expand for me my [spiritual] chest."[58]

Intellectual Characteristics

As for the intellectual characteristics of a preacher, first off one should have: proficiency of scholarship (*tafaqquh*). Not only is seeking knowledge incumbent upon everyone, but gaining expertise and an in depth proficiency of scholarship is a prerequisite for one to teach others. The Qur'an states:

﴿فَلَوْلَا نَفَرَ مِن كُلِّ فِرْقَةٍ مِّنْهُمْ طَائِفَةٌ لِّيَتَفَقَّهُوا فِي الدِّينِ وَلِيُنذِرُوا قَوْمَهُمْ إِذَا رَجَعُوا إِلَيْهِمْ لَعَلَّهُمْ يَحْذَرُونَ﴾

> "When then does not a contingent from among each group of believers remain behind to devote themselves to the in-depth study in matters of the religion so that when the other members of their community return back to them, they may warn them?"[59]

Educating the masses on various topics related to Islam requires a solid scholarly foundation so that confusion in preaching and teaching is avoided. Scholarship ensures that the information one is passing along to others is accurate and reliable. Unfortunately, it may be observed

[58] Qur'an, Sūrah Ṭāhā (20), verse 25.
[59] Qur'an, Sūrah al-Tawbah (9), verse 122.

sometimes that a lack of education on part of a preacher has dire consequences, resulting in misinformation and confusion.

The second intellectual characteristic is a commitment to the continuity and sustainability of knowledge. It is not enough for a preacher to gain expertise and scholarship, but one must continue to advance one's education. This includes making sure that one's presentations, lectures, and discussions are fully prepared, so as not to waste the time of audiences and community members. The preacher must be well-versed, professional, and have a strong command of the areas of teaching. One must not be superficial, and thus it requires a thorough and continuous research and development. The Qur'an states:

﴿قُلْ هَٰذِهِ سَبِيلِي أَدْعُو إِلَى اللَّهِ عَلَىٰ بَصِيرَةٍ﴾

> "Say [Muḥammad]: this is my way, I invite unto God with deep insight."[60]

Furthermore, the preacher must have breadth of knowledge also. Generic information is not enough, but rather, they must be specific, exhaustive, and elaborative as well. Imam ʿAlī states: "Do not state what you do not know, otherwise you will be (deemed) suspicious even when you speak about what you know."[61] If a preacher is not comprehensive, then will be committing an injustice to not only themselves, but more importantly, to the subject matter, because this may cause rejection of the doctrine or subject completely.

As an example, we notice that the prophets were accused of being followed only by fools and those who were superficial and "immature in judgment":

[60] Qur'an, Sūrah Yūsuf (12), verse 108.
[61] Al-Āmidī, *Ghurar al-Ḥikam*, maxim 274.

﴿فَقَالَ الْمَلَأُ الَّذِينَ كَفَرُوا مِنْ قَوْمِهِ مَا نَرَاكَ إِلَّا بَشَرًا مِثْلَنَا وَمَا نَرَاكَ اتَّبَعَكَ إِلَّا الَّذِينَ هُمْ أَرَاذِلُنَا بَادِيَ الرَّأْيِ وَمَا نَرَىٰ لَكُمْ عَلَيْنَا مِنْ فَضْلٍ بَلْ نَظُنُّكُمْ كَاذِبِينَ﴾

> "But the chiefs of those who disbelieved from among his people said: We do not consider you but a mortal like ourselves, and we do not see any have followed you but those who are the meanest of us at first thought and we do not see in you any excellence over us; nay, we deem you liars."[62]

The implication of this was that the prophets' ideas were shallow and unconvincing. As an educator, one must acquire the ability of deducing *furūʿ* (derivatives) from the *uṣūl* (principles); but often times preachers have difficulty applying the principles. On the other hand, sometimes a preacher is aware of the derivatives, but is not able to connect them to the principles.

Thirdly, an educator must be well connected to various areas of knowledge and understanding besides theology, such as those concerning the political, social, economic, and other aspects of life. This is especially important because preachers in the west are required to connect Islamic theology, law, and ethics to everyday life. Islam is a holistic religion and is not confined to theological or philosophical debates. Its purpose is to provide guidance for every aspect of life, and as such, it is imperative that the preacher and educator is well versed in other sciences and fields of education as well.

Practical Characteristics

As for the practical characteristics, a preacher must possess: oratory skills, eloquence, and the ability to convey one's message to the masses appropriately and effectively. It may be observed that some educators possess adequate knowledge, but lack the skills to convey them, or vice versa. Effective preaching requires both comprehensive and in depth

---

[62] Qur'an, Sūrah Hūd (11), verse 27.

knowledge, as well as effective communication skills, for these two are inseparable. On this note, the Qur'an relays Prophet Moses's request from God:

﴿وَاحْلُلْ عُقْدَةً مِّن لِّسَانِي يَفْقَهُوا قَوْلِي﴾

"And remove the impediment from my speech, so they may understand what I say."[63]

Acquiring effective oratory skills requires practice and the study of various techniques for dynamic communication.

The second practical characteristic for a preacher is the ability to convince the audiences through the power of reasoning and academic presentation of material. The Qur'an reminds us about this sort of delivery and argumentation when it states:

﴿وَجَادِلْهُم بِالَّتِي هِيَ أَحْسَنُ﴾

"And argue with them in the most appropriate method."[64]

This is especially important in the West, where there is an emphasis on reasoning, rather than blind imitation. An educator cannot present one's materials and expect the audiences to accept them uncritically and without question. Therefore, one must be well prepared to present convincing and reasonable evidence and analysis for any educational material.

Thirdly, educators must realize the interconnectedness of this world - that the world is now a global village. The preacher must be able to engage in discussions which are not based purely on religious issues and to take the circumstances and contexts of society into consideration.

Finally, preachers must possess adequate awareness of particular challenges and needs of every demographic group in society (youth, men, women, children, students, merchants, etc.). As such, they must avoid being too general in their speeches, and rather be able to delve

---

[63] Qur'an, Sūrah Ṭāhā (20), verses 27-28.
[64] Qur'an, Sūrah al-Naḥl (16), verse 125.

deeply into addressing the specific issues related to that particular group and their needs.

Interfaith Dialogue

Among the greatest types of social relationships in the United States of America are created and developed through interfaith dialogue. However, it must be noted that in the context of America and the West, the goal behind this type of dialogue is not necessarily to convert one another, but to better understand each other. This goal is clearly defined in the Holy Qur'an:

﴿يَا أَيُّهَا النَّاسُ إِنَّا خَلَقْنَاكُم مِّن ذَكَرٍ وَأُنثَىٰ وَجَعَلْنَاكُمْ شُعُوبًا وَقَبَائِلَ لِتَعَارَفُوا﴾

> "O humanity, surely We have created you from a male and female, and made you into nations and tribes so that you may recognize one another."[65]

Interfaith dialogue refers to positive interaction between adherents of different faiths with the goal of finding a common ground in principles and values among the religious traditions. It is also used to achieve further understanding and cooperation between adherents of different faiths in order to create an equal and diverse society which honors and upholds peace, love, openness, and stability in the world.

Muslims have benefited from their experiences in interfaith dialogue, because it has cleared up much of the misconceptions that surround Islam; especially Islam's stance on world peace, other faiths, democracy, freedom, women's role in society, and other issues. Many leaders of other faiths have admitted that they have benefited from interfaith dialogue with Muslims, as their own misconceptions on Islam have been cleared up through them.

Among the most important results from interfaith dialogue is that religious leaders stand by the side of Muslims and support them

---

[65] Qur'an, Sūrah al-Ḥujurāt (49), verse 13.

through turbulent times, especially in the face of attacks from those who intend to subdue Muslims with accusations of extremism and attempt to replace American law with sharīʿah law. Churches and other religious institutions in many cases stood to defend their Muslim neighbors against racial discrimination in the wake of the September 11th, 2001 terrorist attacks. They stood in front of mosques and Islamic schools in defense of the attacks and threats from extremists, issued statements denouncing the desecration of Islamic centers, and reinforced their support for laws which ensure equal rights and privileges for Muslims in the face of extremist calls to prevent Muslims from participating in the political and social sphere.

History of Interfaith Dialogue

The history of Islamic interfaith dialogue is as old as religion itself. The dialogue between the Holy Prophet and the Christians of Najrān may have been the first Muslim-Christian dialogue of its time.

Some historians consider the dialogue between the Prophet and the Christian leaders of Najrān as an opportunity for the latter to understand the principles in Islam, which led to their retraction from the mutual execration (*mubāhalah*) with the Prophet and his progeny, and their return to Najrān. This then led to their eventual return to Medina to accept Islam based on understanding and conviction.

Subsequently, dialogue sessions between Muslims and adherents of other faiths continued through the era of the Caliphs, with Imam ʿAlī ibn Abī Tālib spearheading the dialogue which would take place between the Jews and Christians on one end, and the Muslims on the other end. His replies were always sufficient enough to answer the inquiries of those asking. Many of these debates have been recorded in the book *al-Iḥtijāj* by al-Ṭabrasi, the famous fourteenth century Shīʿa scholar.

Among the eras in which stability between Islam and other faiths flourished as a result of interfaith dialogue was that of Al-Andalus (Islamic Spain). This was known as the Golden Age because of the theological and religious diversity, which was uncommon in human history. This paved the way for the opportunity for further dialogue, which fluctuated depending on political stability, war, and civil strife.

It is interesting to note that ironically some conflicts have become the reason behind some world religious leaders in initiating and reviving faith-based dialogue. Many cultural and religious dialogue institutions have been established as a result, as well as centers for Muslim-Christian understanding in Europe and North America at important schools through Muslim-Christian funding. Among the latest initiatives is one that is named "A Common Word Between Us and You."

Personal Observations on Interfaith Dialogue

From over two decades of experience in the field of interfaith dialogue, a few observations have been analyzed by this author that seem useful to include in this work.

Through our meetings and mutual dialogue, I have found that some Jewish Rabbis are sympathetic to their Muslim peers while showing respect to the Islamic faith. They sympathize with Muslim causes, especially confronting Islamophobia and racial discrimination towards Muslims. On the other hand, I have also found that some religious leaders are open about their animosity towards Muslims. This is apparent from their public statements in the media and from their treatment of Islamic leaders and institutions, as they consider all Muslims as extremists and radicals who pose a danger to the security of the United States and the world.

Here we learn an important lesson: Not to generalize all non-Muslims as hateful towards Islam. Some religious leaders, churches, and synagogues respect Muslims and sympathize with them; while others openly express their animosity towards Muslims and their beliefs; and some others respect Muslims, but do not respect Islam. Few also respect Islam as a faith but not Muslims, because they cannot tolerate their behavior and character.

The recent civilization which has emerged in the West has caused a reexamination in its method of thinking and dealing with others. People have now become more tolerant and accepting of different views. Recent surveys have shown that Americans are now searching for faiths or beliefs which may answer their questions on God and the values of life.

A contemporary study by Pew suggested that 5 in every 10 Americans have changed their faith from one to another.[66] It is not uncommon for someone to find a single household with multiple faiths and beliefs and in fact, I was told by a person at an interfaith event in Windsor, Canada, that his family of five consists of five adherents to five different faiths: Islam, Christianity, Judaism, Buddhism, and Gnosticism!

In another session, I listened to a woman during an Orange County, California interfaith event who left Catholicism for Buddhism and she talked about her 'experience' with a Catholic priest, and he stayed listening to her without anger or accusation of apostasy. In fact, he referred to her as his partner in interfaith dialogue. This proves that the zealous religious sentiment which exists in the Middle East does not necessarily exist in the West, and this is a result of civility and tolerance towards others.

Some may ask the question: How is it that a person who engages in interfaith dialogue with leaders of other faiths can repeatedly listen to claims of other faiths, such as those concerning the Trinity, the hypostatic union, and the Old and New Testaments which attribute "blasphemies" to the prophets, and not react to these claims?! This is an important question, but before answering it, let us examine the following: There are some Muslim leaders in the West who believe that there is no point or benefit from engaging in interfaith dialogue. This is because theological and foundational differences are not discussed, and most of the time is spent discussing minor unimportant issues and listening to texts containing blasphemy, heresy, and innovations, which pose a moral problem. These Muslim leaders believe that Islam teaches us to actively confront belief systems which deny monotheism, associate partners with God, or go against Islamic teachings. Again,

[66] http://www.pewforum.org/2009/04/27/faith-in-flux/. Visited January 1, 2016.

this is the opinion of some Muslims scholars, and some of them live in the West.

Most others believe that the goal behind participating in interfaith dialogue does not mean that one has to accept others' beliefs, but it means to familiarize others with Islam and the correct foundations of oneness, which was propagated by all the prophets and messengers, beginning with Prophet Abraham. Likewise, the goal behind interfaith dialogue is not about conversion as much as it is about removing misconceptions about Islam. This group sees that Muslims are the ones to benefit from this type of dialogue, as it weakens the severity of the up-hill battles which Muslims constantly have to face.

What Muslims in the West suffer from today is not small numbers or insufficient funds and resources, but the organized Islamophobic campaign initiated by entities against Muslim presence in the West.

There are groups who believe that Muslims do not have the right to live in Europe or North America, for they are foreign to these lands, and that the United States is exclusively for people of the Judeo-Christian background and no one else! It seems that the Western civilization came a long way in its religious and racial tolerance, but has limited this level of tolerance to only select religions.

This is why we see conservative right-wing Christians calling for the rescue of Christians in places like Egypt, Sudan, Lebanon, and Iraq from *takfīrīs*, while completely ignoring the prejudice facing Muslim communities in Europe and North America in building mosques, observing ḥijāb, in schools and in national security administrations.

Tolerance is weighed on two different scales: The privileges that apply to non-Muslims don't apply to Muslims, and the persecution which is prohibited against non-Muslims is allowed on others. Studies have shown that breaches against Muslim civil liberties have risen in the United States of America, and that it is related to a rise in Islamophobia in America. This is why interfaith dialogue is an important component in minimizing these campaigns, while also educating adherents of other faiths about the peaceful nature of Islam

Among the most famous of attempts to destabilize the existence of Islam in America was the Peter King Hearings which took place in the Spring of 2011.

Peter King was a Republican Representative of Congress from New York, and the chairperson of the House Homeland Security Committee. He is known for his anti-Islamic remarks, and has been attributed as saying that there are "too many mosques in America" and that "85% of mosques in this country are controlled by Islamic fundamentalists ... This is an enemy living amongst us." He also claimed that Muslim communities do not support the government like other communities do.

These remarks resulted in a wave of anti-Islamic attacks in the media, as Muslims feared for their security and future. These attempts however failed, due to the commitment of the leaders of religious communities alongside the Muslim communities to stand shoulder to shoulder in defense of American Muslims. This partnership evolved into an organization comprised of the National Council of Churches in America, the Council of Catholic Bishops, as well as five major Jewish organizations and other members.

It is safe to conclude that this is one of the fruits bore by interfaith dialogue in the United States of America. Muslims today are in need of non-Muslim voices which will defend them, for they are more powerful and influential among Americans in this regard. Peter King initiated these hearings based on some claims that American Muslims do not cooperate with Law Enforcement, but what he found was that the most senior Law Enforcement official in Los Angeles, Sheriff Lee Baca, praised the efforts of the Muslim community in cooperating with Law enforcement officials to fight terror.

This is one story among many which reiterates the importance of having peaceful relationships with other faiths and communities, which result in important stances during hard times.

It is no doubt that the participation of Muslims in interfaith dialogue requires certain elements, and I believe that this type of activity is not for all Islamic educators. Apart from having knowledge, wisdom, and articulation, one must also know how to be considerate when facing things which may be blasphemous or unappealing. Respect, tolerance, and the ability to show the appealing side of Islam during modern times is very crucial.

From personal experiences in daʿwah and tablīgh, I have found that most people who accept Islam do so because of the Islamic stance on ethics, tolerance, wisdom, intellect, and mercy. What brought them to Islam was not the philosophical or theological debates between Islam and other faiths, but rather the spirit of equality and justice in Islam. This is why faith and ethics are on the same level of importance to one another within individuals and society; but in matters of tablīgh, ethics outweigh faith. Here, we see the significance of the traditions which emphasize the importance of inviting others to faith through actions and not through words.

If Christianity believes that Prophet Jesus is the manifestation of the Lord in this world, and that he came to teach people mercy and forgiveness, then Islam believes that a believer is the vicegerent of God on Earth, and that God has endowed the human being with a pristine message with the intention that with this message a person is able to reach the highest levels of perfection. With this, one is able to achieve the desire of God and His will for mankind, and achieve the goal that one was created for.

The Most Controversial Topics between Muslims and non-Muslims

There are a number of topics that dominate the various discussions that arise between Muslims and non-Muslims. Among the most important ones are: Women's rights, freedom of religion, apostasy, *jihād* (sacred struggle), violence and terrorism, and Islam's stance towards adherents of other religions such as the Jews, as in the verse of the Qurʾan found in chapter 5, verse 82:

﴿لَتَجِدَنَّ أَشَدَّ النَّاسِ عَدَاوَةً لِّلَّذِينَ آمَنُوا الْيَهُودَ وَالَّذِينَ أَشْرَكُوا ۖ
وَلَتَجِدَنَّ أَقْرَبَهُم مَّوَدَّةً لِّلَّذِينَ آمَنُوا الَّذِينَ قَالُوا إِنَّا نَصَارَىٰ ۚ ذَٰلِكَ بِأَنَّ
مِنْهُمْ قِسِّيسِينَ وَرُهْبَانًا وَأَنَّهُمْ لَا يَسْتَكْبِرُونَ﴾

> "You shall certainly find the Jews and those who associate partners with God the most vehement of the people in enmity against those who believe, and you shall certainly find those who say, 'We are Christians,' the nearest in friendship towards those who believe. That is so because there are savants and monks amongst them and because they are not haughty."

And the polytheists, as is seen in the Qur'an in chapter 9, verse 5:

﴿فَإِذَا انسَلَخَ الْأَشْهُرُ الْحُرُمُ فَاقْتُلُوا الْمُشْرِكِينَ حَيْثُ وَجَدتُّمُوهُمْ
وَخُذُوهُمْ وَاحْصُرُوهُمْ وَاقْعُدُوا لَهُمْ كُلَّ مَرْصَدٍ ۚ فَإِن تَابُوا وَأَقَامُوا
الصَّلَاةَ وَآتَوُا الزَّكَاةَ فَخَلُّوا سَبِيلَهُمْ ۚ إِنَّ اللَّهَ غَفُورٌ رَّحِيمٌ﴾

> "But when the prohibited (four) months (when no attack on the breakers of the treaties was permissible) have expired, slay such polytheists (who broke their treaties) wherever you find them and capture them and besiege them and lie in wait for them in every place from which it is possible to perceive the enemy and watch their movements. But if they turn in repentance and keep up prayer and go on presenting the charity tax (*zakāt*), leave their path free. Indeed, God is Great Protector, Ever Merciful."

Some outsiders point the finger towards Islam as a religion that supports and encourages violence, animosity, and the murder of innocent people. They claim that there is no place for love and tolerance of opposing views in Islam, and that it confronts opposition with severity and harshness. These ideas are frequently relayed in the media, through religious leaders and organizations, activists, academics, entertainers, and politicians across North America and Europe. In America, such stereotypes are employed especially before elections during political campaigns as a means to achieve political victory against opponents.

The reply to these ideas are based on two major points: First, it is essential to understand that when we read a religious text, we must **not** overlook the historical and theological context, and we need to take into consideration the circumstances that revolved around the situation or occasion before interpretation. It is unfair and illogical to quote a verse, or remove it from its historical context or correct frame. When we mention the prior verses (5:82 and 9:5) or others from the Qurʾan, or we quote a *Ḥadīth* we must read them within the appropriate context, and refrain from fabricating, altering, and misinterpreting the text. This requires a serious observation of the wordings, one that is not is as simple as reading over it and passing simple judgment on it.

Thus, in the case of Islam's stance towards the Jews, such as in 5:82 of the Qurʾan, we find that Islam does not criticize Jews simply for their ethnicity or for being followers of Prophet Moses. This cannot be the case, because the Qurʾan repeatedly emphasizes the high status of Prophet Moses, the prophets of *banī isrā'īl*, and the *Torah* and its laws, such as the verse:

﴿إِنَّا أَنزَلْنَا التَّوْرَاةَ فِيهَا هُدًى وَنُورٌ يَحْكُمُ بِهَا النَّبِيُّونَ الَّذِينَ أَسْلَمُوا لِلَّذِينَ هَادُوا وَالرَّبَّانِيُّونَ وَالْأَحْبَارُ بِمَا اسْتُحْفِظُوا مِن كِتَابِ اللَّهِ وَكَانُوا عَلَيْهِ شُهَدَاءَ﴾

"Surely We have revealed the Torah, wherein is guidance and light. The prophets who submitted [to God] judged the Jews according to it, so did the rabbis and the scholars, as they were required to protect God's Book, and they were witnesses to it."[67]

We also find that the Qur'an commands the Muslims to be benevolent towards the People of the Book [the Jews and Christians] who do not take a negative stance against the Muslims:

﴿لَّا يَنْهَاكُمُ اللَّهُ عَنِ الَّذِينَ لَمْ يُقَاتِلُوكُمْ فِي الدِّينِ وَلَمْ يُخْرِجُوكُم مِّن دِيَارِكُمْ أَن تَبَرُّوهُمْ وَتُقْسِطُوا إِلَيْهِمْ إِنَّ اللَّهَ يُحِبُّ الْمُقْسِطِينَ﴾

"God does not forbid you from those who do not fight you because of religion and do not expel you from your homes - from being righteous towards them and acting justly towards them. Indeed, God loves those who act justly."[68]

In the verse in question (5:82), God is describing the Jews that stood against the Prophet in enmity and deception, and against his newly introduced message, and conspired and planned to fight against Islam in order to eradicate it. This harsh Qur'anic description is not only used against those Jews, but even against some hypocrites within the Islamic community in Mecca and Medina. Among the hypocrites were some from the Prophet's own family members, because they chose this life over the next and stood beside evil against the truth.

Thus, the Qur'anic reprimand towards the non-Muslims does not originate from animosity or prejudicial grudges. The Qur'an reinforces those who support truth and justice; but on the other hand, stands against and rebukes those who encourage falsehood and oppression - whoever they may be.

Secondly, many verses in the Old and New Testaments speak about destruction, violence, death, captivity, and subjugation. However, Islam does not allow us to accuse the Jews and Christians and their holy books or prophets as instigators of violence, destruction, and oppression. For instance, we read passages in the Old Testament which

---

[67] Qur'an, Sūrah al-Mā'idah (5), verse 44.
[68] Qur'an, Sūrah al-Mumtahanah (60), verse 8.

may lead a simple reader to believe that the text supports murder and bloodshed. However, an objective reader will try to find an interpretation to these passages and understand the historical and theological contexts and circumstances surrounding it.

In Deuteronomy 32:42, we find that Prophet Moses speaks to his Lord before entering the Holy Land, and said: "I will make mine arrows drunk with blood, and my sword shall devour flesh, and that with the blood of the slain and of the captives from the beginning of revenges upon the enemy."

In Deuteronomy 7:1-2, Prophet Moses instructed the Israelites (*banī isrā'īl*) on what to do with the captives, saying: "And when the Lord your God has delivered them over to you and you have defeated them, then you must destroy them totally. Make no treaty with them, and show them no mercy."

In Numbers 31:17-18, we find Prophet Moses instructing his soldiers to use aggression against women and children by saying: "Now kill all the boys. And kill every woman who has slept with a man, but save for yourselves every girl who has never slept with a man."

There are many verses like these in the Old Testament. Similar harsh verses can be found in the New Testament. In the Book of Matthew 10:34-35, we read the words of Prophet Jesus: "Do not suppose that I have come to bring peace to the earth. I did not come to bring peace, but a sword. I have come to turn a man against his father, a daughter against her mother, a daughter-in-law against her mother-in-law."

In addition, in Luke 19:27, the following statement is attributed to Prophet Jesus: "But those enemies of mine who did not want me to be king over them – bring them here and kill them in front of me." Other verses similar to these are found in the New Testament.

Despite all of this, the Islamic outlook on the prophets and their divine messages does not falter and is in contrast with these words which are attributed to them. Our belief is that all of the prophets, from Adam to Muḥammad, are immaculate and error-free; they are immune against any sins and erring. Our belief is that all divine messages were delivered for the sake of the betterment of humanity, and to spread peace, justice, guidance, and love among the believers. The message of every prophet was to complete the message of the one before him, and the messages of all of their books were in sync with one another, and their message was the same; the recognition of God and His oneness, to worship Him, and to abstain from polytheism, hatred, envy, and jealousy. Their work was to restore honor to humankind, confront the oppressors, aid the oppressed, and successfully pass through the temporary station of this life to the permanent station of the afterlife.

Contemporary Challenges of Churches in the West

Churches in the West today do not have the same influence that they once had. Today, the church has lost a lot of its prior authority and control that it previously had; control which for centuries had the ability to govern kings, scientists, and leaders alike.

Due to the corruption of the men of the European churches, there came calls to reform and to have freedom for religious control. Among the most well-known of those attempts was that of Martin Luther (d. 1546) from Germany and elsewhere, which was knows as the Protestant reformation; because they believed that they should not be governed except by the Holy Book, they became known as the Evangelists.

This movement spread across Europe and reached the United States. Among their objectives was to translate the Bible to contemporary languages so that people would understand the language of the Evangel and be affected by it. They also abandoned many of the Catholic rituals such as priesthood, confession to priests, placing sculptures and pictures and prostrating to them.

From there, many sects and denominations, such as the Baptists, Quakers, and Calvinists began to emerge as they gradually departed from Catholicism. These separations caused many conflicts and battles between Protestants and Catholics in the mid-seventeenth century and lasted for thirty years. Some of these conflicts continue in countries such as Ireland, Spain, and other places.

Western churches, with all of their denominations, face two main types of challenges: the first is the problem of diminishing faith, and the second is the problem of moral decay.

The problem of diminishing faith exists because Christianity has not been able to keep up with the intellectual and scientific evolution of society.

The church has relied upon traditional teachings which have not provided logical and clear answers to those the seeking truth, for many of the churches symbols are paganistic and do not represent the true teachings of Prophet Jesus. Many of the ideas, such as the trinity, hypostatic union, baptizing, crucifixion, and confession, do not comply with today's intellectual evolution. For this reason, the Western churches have made bargains in order to make their beliefs more acceptable to the masses.

Churches in the United States have begun to revise much of their beliefs and traditions to meet the demands of modernization and become more palatable with people and their beliefs. They allowed women to the position of priesthood and leadership in the church, they allowed homosexuals to be a part of the church and even lead the people, and some allowed for music bands to perform inside the church. Attending Mass did not have to be in modest clothing, and establishing churches became a way to affluence, riches, and fame. Some important churches even fell apart due to financial corruption.

As for the second problem, the moral decay of members and priests of the church, we find that the Catholic Church in the United States has spent millions of dollars as compensation for victims of sexual abuse for many years all across the country. This kind of abuse was left unspoken about for several years, and many of the victims were children and young boys, who were abused by the priests. This type of behavior led to people losing their trust in the church and its ability to solve peoples' problems and provide them with spiritual meaning. It also led to many Catholics abandoning their faith and going towards other churches and religions.

The Protestant church is not free from problems either. Allegations of sexual abuse and misconduct from protestant ministers and leaders towards children and women in return for money have been made. The money was given in return for the victims' silence. This type of behavior led to waves of abandonment of the churches in the West, as the church lost much of its spiritual and ethical importance among the people. Today it is treated as any other institution and moves towards secularism and away from religiosity.

Why and How Americans Convert to Islam

Most Americans tend to have a non-dogmatic approach to faith.[69] Many believe that truth and eternal salvation are not exclusive to their own religious traditions, but may be achieved within other religious traditions as well.

These two factors, along with freedom of religion, have produced an appropriate foundation for Americans to pursue and embrace various religious traditions, including Islam. In the United States, despite rising Islamophobia and anti-Muslim rhetoric, Islam continues to grow. By 2030, the population of Muslims in America is expected to double in size and encompass various demographics groups.[70] In addition to the immigrant and American born Muslims, approximately 23% of the Muslim population in America is composed of converts to Islam.[71] In addition, Americans are converting to Islam for various reasons. But arguably it seems that the primary reason behind the conversion of many Americans to Islam is the appeal of the religion's moral, ethical, and social values.

During my conversations with many American converts to Islam, I have constantly been informed that the primary reason for their conversion has been the noble values and morals that Islam presents. Many of the converts have been attracted to Islam through instances

---

69 See *U.S. Religious Landscape Survey (2008)*, The Pew Forum on Religion and Public Life, pg. 4.
70 http://www.pewforum.org/2011/01/27/the-future-of-the-global-muslim-population/#the-americas. Visited January 1, 2016.
71 http://www.pewresearch.org/daily-number/converts-to-Islam/. Visited January 1, 2016.

in which they have experienced respect, generosity, nobility, humility, and kindness from Muslim neighbors, co-workers, and friends.

For example, I was once participating in a conference on Islam in St. Louis, Missouri. There, a young man approached me and we had a discussion in which he informed me that he had converted to Islam as a result of the spectacular generosity that he witnessed by his Muslim neighbors who had recently emigrated from Iraq.

Another example is of a young woman who attended our Islamic Educational Center of Orange County's annual summer youth camp and informed the participants that, after spending three full days with them, she came to realize that Muslims do indeed practice their Qurʾanic injunctions of respect, compassion, and cooperation, and as such, she decided to embrace Islam at that moment.

There are many other instances and examples of converts who embraced Islam because of the special social and ethical values that the faith encourages and instructs its adherents on observing. Of course, we are reminded that one of the most important methods of daʿwah is through our noble actions and interactions, as taught by Imam al-Ṣādiq: "Call to us without the use of your tongues."[72]

The common perception about proselytization and conversion to Islam is that the younger generation and the less educated make up the majority of the converts, and conversions are primarily based on emotional reasons with no intellectual foundation. Although not all converts are intellectuals and they comprise of various demographic groups, however, the conversion of many intellectuals is also a matter of fact. We see this in the case of various intellectuals, academics, scholars, and community leaders who have converted to Islam due to its intellectual and scholarly appeal.

The Appeal of Sufism

In recent decades, there has been a rising trend of attraction among many Americans towards Sufism. Over the course of approximately two centuries of the study of Sufism in the West, a plethora of

---

[72] *Al-Kāfī*, v. 2, p. 78.

translations, analyses, histories, and expositions of Sufi works have appeared and have become increasingly accessible to western readers. One reason for this rise in interest of Sufism is due to Sufism itself: Sufis are highly organized, well-resourced, and extremely diligent and enthusiastic in presenting their ideas and experiences to others. Additionally, a number of highly regarded scholars and academics have promoted Sufism to westerners. Some of the most important works in this regard include *Sufism: Veil and Quintessence* by Frithjof Schuon, *What is Sufism?* by Martin Lings; and *The Garden of Truth* by Seyyed Hossein Nasr. A vast number of Sufi literature has been translated into multiple languages and are considered to be best-sellers. For instance, the thirteenth century Persian poet and mystic Jalāl al-Dīn Rūmī, continues to be the most popular poet in the United States with millions of his works sold annually.

A second reason is due to the fact that a significant number of Americans suffer from spiritual emptiness, as a result of their focus on materialism. This is evident by the significant number of Americans who suffer from depression and anxiety, and are addicted to alcohol, illicit drugs, and prescription drugs. Thus, Americans are attracted towards spiritual (metaphysical) language. Sufism's strong suit has an ability to express spiritual appeal to the masses. In the words of Seyyed Hossein Nasr, he states: "Sufism is a vast reality that provides the means for those who follow its tenets to reach the Garden of Truth. It is the path to the Garden and, on the highest level and in its inner reality, the "content" of the Garden as well as the means of reaching the Presence of the Gardner ... above all, it can enable men and women to reach the state of sanctity."[73]

Furthermore, Seyyed Hossein Nasr argues that Sufism plays a crucial role in the encounters and dialogue between Islam and other religions: "In the West [Sufism] is the most accessible means for understanding Islam in its essential reality."[74] Perhaps this may be because Sufism focuses on the "spiritual" more so than it does on the

---

[73] Nasr, Seyyed Hossein, *The Garden of Truth: The Vision and Promise of Ṣufism, Islam's Mystical Tradition*, p. xv.

[74] Ibid., p. xvi.

"religious", and as such, provides a common platform for interreligious dialogue and understanding.

In the words of imam Jamal Rahman, a popular Sufi interreligious minister in America, "Sufis are Muslims who emphasize essence over form and substance over appearance in their spiritual practices. If the institution of religion can be compared to a cup and the water in it is the spiritual message, Sufis lament that we spend too much time polishing the outside of the cup and neglect to drink the water. They do subscribe to outer rituals, but are mostly eager to do the inner work. They aspire to taste and live the essence of their faith."[75]

Another noteworthy reason why there is a general appeal among Americans towards Sufism is because essentially, Sufism focuses solely on the connection of humans to God, distancing itself from various forms of politics. Americans are attracted to this separation of church and state and privatization of faith and religion in their lives. This version of Islam (the apolitical focus on spirituality) works well for Americans, and does not pose any danger for them. Thus, Sufism is able to thrive because it does not clash with western secular values and does not pose a threat to what some Americans seem to assume exists under political forms and expressions of Islam.

Intra-Faith Dialogue

Shīʿa-Sunnī relations are different in the West than they are in the Middle East. In the Middle East, these relations are for the most part, characterized by mistrust and instability. However in the West, these relations are for the most part, built upon respect, understanding, and cooperation. This does not mean that we are completely content with this relation - we should strive for their advancement. There have also been exceptions to these rules. In the past, there have been confrontations and skirmish between the two sects in the United States. Sometimes, there is a disregard for each other's activities and achievements; however, this should not prevent the leaders of the two schools of thought from treating each other with respect and honor.

[75] Rahman, Jamal, *Spiritual Gems of Islam*, p. xiii.

There have been sincere attempts to bring the two together through meetings, conferences, and general activities. However, these attempts are new and in need of continuation and advancement.

There are a few obstacles which stand in the way of unity between the different schools of thought in America, such as the legacy that old sectarian conflicts have left behind in people's minds, especially because most Muslims in America are from the immigrant class, and this generation represents the largest of those who seek out conflicts to use against one another.

Another factor is the foreign intervention by some Middle Eastern governments in American Muslim matters. They have supported mosques and institutions across Europe and North America; and we know that support comes with strings and conditions attached.

Some of these conditions include the expulsion of Muslims from different schools of thought, fabricating lies against other schools of thought, accusing them of innovation, *takfīr* (anathematization); and prohibiting them from marrying one another, eating each other's food, and donating and praying with one another. This happened to me in Seattle, where I was asked by the Iraqi Sunnī Imam of a masjid to lead the noon prayers and lecture after it. I respectfully declined to lead the prayers, but I agreed to speak after it. When I stood to speak about the importance of unity and cooperation, two Salafī men, one Egyptian and the other Algerian, stood up and interrupted me and began to accuse me of heresy and threatened to expel me from the masjid because I was a "disbeliever." All this happened while the imam was pleading with them to stop their attacks and respect the sanctity of the masjid. This incident occurred in the heart of America, in broad daylight, and in front of other worshippers. This shows the extent of the ferocity of this narrow type of thinking and how it is being supported by some foreign Islamic governments.

Among the other obstacles in the way of Islamic unity in the West is the limited degree of Islamic awareness and enlightenment for most community members. Although we see that the Islamic community enjoys a high level of awareness and understanding in terms of general sciences, however this level of understanding diminishes when it comes to Islamic awareness. Communities depend on the heritage they received from their schools of thought, without going through the trouble and making the effort of getting to know one another. It hurts to see that leaders of some schools of thought are open to outsiders, especially People of the Book, but when it comes to intra-faith dialogue, the effort remains unattended to and ignored.

Some extremists have requested that the Shīʿa be expelled from Sunnī mosques, but on the other hand they remain open to other religions. This is because they perceive an ideological threat from Shīʿas, but not from people of other religions.

A Call for Unity between Muslims

The ideal type of unity between people described in the Qur'an occurs in three stages: First, unity between humankind. The Qur'an describes this world as a small village, and that people in it are equal in creation and responsibility, and it invites them to cooperation to protect the coming generations and to protect the earth from destruction:

﴿يَا أَيُّهَا النَّاسُ إِنَّا خَلَقْنَاكُم مِّن ذَكَرٍ وَأُنثَىٰ وَجَعَلْنَاكُمْ شُعُوبًا وَقَبَائِلَ لِتَعَارَفُوا إِنَّ أَكْرَمَكُمْ عِندَ اللَّهِ أَتْقَاكُمْ إِنَّ اللَّهَ عَلِيمٌ خَبِيرٌ﴾

> "O mankind, we have created you from a male and a female, and made you into races and tribes, so that you may identify one another. Surely, the noblest of you in God's sight, is the one who is the most pious among you. Indeed God is All-Knowing, All-Aware"[76]

With this golden rule, the Qur'an fights against racial segregation and nationalism, and focuses on equality between humanity.

---

[76] Qur'an, Sūrah al-Ḥujurāt (49), verse 13.

The second type is unity between adherents of monotheistic faiths. The Qur'an invites the People of the Book to unity based on the principles of true monotheism and accurate beliefs in God. It says:

﴿قُلْ يَا أَهْلَ الْكِتَابِ تَعَالَوْا إِلَىٰ كَلِمَةٍ سَوَاءٍ بَيْنَنَا وَبَيْنَكُمْ أَلَّا نَعْبُدَ إِلَّا اللَّهَ وَلَا نُشْرِكَ بِهِ شَيْئًا﴾

> "Say [Muḥammad]: O People of the Book, come to a common word between us and between you, that we worship none except God and that we associate nothing with Him..."[77]

This type of unity is built on the foundations and pillars of faith, not on details and rites. The Qur'an emphasizes that:

﴿لِكُلٍّ جَعَلْنَا مِنكُمْ شِرْعَةً وَمِنْهَاجًا﴾

> "For each of you we have made a law and a method."[78]

The third type of unity is that within the Islamic community. The Qur'an invites Muslims to hold steadfast to the rope of God:

﴿وَاعْتَصِمُوا بِحَبْلِ اللَّهِ جَمِيعًا وَلَا تَفَرَّقُوا﴾

> "And hold fast, all of you, to the cord of God, and do not be divided."[79]

The Qur'an also invites Muslims towards brotherhood and reconcilement:

﴿إِنَّمَا الْمُؤْمِنُونَ إِخْوَةٌ فَأَصْلِحُوا بَيْنَ أَخَوَيْكُمْ ۚ وَاتَّقُوا اللَّهَ لَعَلَّكُمْ تُرْحَمُونَ﴾

[77] Qur'an, Sūrah Āle 'Imrān (3), verse 64.
[78] Qur'an, Sūrah al-Mā'idah (5), verse 48.
[79] Qur'an, Sūrah Āle 'Imrān (3), verse 103.

"All believers are but brothers, therefore seek reconciliation between your two brothers, and fear God, so that you may be blessed with mercy."[80]

When the Qur'an speaks about the great prophets and their attributes, it concludes by saying:

﴿إِنَّ هَٰذِهِ أُمَّتُكُمْ أُمَّةً وَاحِدَةً وَأَنَا رَبُّكُمْ فَاعْبُدُونِ﴾

"Surely, this is the fraternity of your community, a single community, and I am your Lord, so worship Me."[81]

All of the messengers, with their divine messages, the holy books, the divine revelations, and the teachings of the prophets, all conclude with the same goals and objectives - that is unity and gathering around monotheism. The final Prophet, in his famous *Ḥadīth al-Thaqalayn* (Tradition of the Two Weighty Objects), [82] commanded his nation to hold on to the book of God and his Progeny (the Ahlulbayt), for they will not separate until they meet at "The Pond," and they are the greatest element and pillar for unity.

From the time that I arrived to the United States as an Islamic educator, I never invited any non-Muslims to convert to Islam, nor any Muslims to accept the Ahlulbayt school of thought, because I do not believe in any value for pushing people to believe in something that they are not fully convinced about. My strategy was to always encourage people to understand Islam through lectures, debates, discussions, and basic literature, and to leave the rest to God. This idea comes from the Qur'anic principle:

---

[80] Qur'an, Sūrah al-Ḥujurāt (49), verse 10.

[81] Qur'an, Sūrah al-Anbiyā' (21), verse 92.

[82] Ḥadīth al-Thaqalayn is one of the most famous traditions narrated from the Holy Prophet. It has been recorded in a large number of Islamic historical and traditional works. Among some of the most important sources for this ḥadīth are: *Ṣaḥīḥ Muslim*, *Musnad Aḥmad ibn Ḥanbal*, *Ṣaḥīḥ al-Tirmidhī*, *al-Mustadrak*, *al-Muṣannaf*, *al-Sunan al-Kubrā*, *Kamāl al-Dīn*, *al-Kāfī*, *al-Mustadrak*, and others.

﴿إِنَّكَ لَا تَهْدِي مَنْ أَحْبَبْتَ وَلَٰكِنَّ اللَّهَ يَهْدِي مَن يَشَاءُ﴾

"Surely You cannot give guidance to whomsoever you wish, but God gives guidance to whomsoever He wills."[83]

By the grace of God and His guidance and blessings, He has honored me by allowing me the means to guide many people to the light of Islam, among them Christians, Jews and others, so that they accepted Islam; as well as to the light of the Prophet and his purified progeny into the hearts of our Muslim brothers, and they have stayed true to their ways by the grace of God. This was all achieved by way of wise and calm dialogue, far from anger, animosity, and rudeness, and based on knowledge, logic, objectivity, and evidence, like it is mentioned in the Qur'an:

﴿قُلْ هَاتُوا بُرْهَانَكُمْ إِن كُنتُمْ صَادِقِينَ﴾

"Say, bring your proof, if you are truthful."[84]

I am extremely pleased today when I witness rows of worshippers during Friday and congregational prayers at our center and other centers across the United States, many of them reverts to Islam and the path of Ahlulbayt. In this, I see clear proof that the path of calmness, wisdom, logic, and extinguishing sectarian conflicts generates positive results. Islam and the school of Ahlulbayt today do not need an increase in quantity, but rather an increase in the quality of adherents. We need an increase in intelligent people who are true to the path of the Prophet, his lifestyle and his teachings; and that of his purified progeny.

I firmly believe that the first element in inviting people to the religion and the Ahlulbayt's school of thought is the element of character and sound Qur'anic conduct. This is what generates true Islamic faith in the hearts of the adherents, and this is what we should preach in the West:

---

83 Qur'an, Sūrah al-Qaṣaṣ (28), verse 56.
84 Qur'an, Sūrah al-Baqarah (2), verse 111.

﴿فَأَمَّا الزَّبَدُ فَيَذْهَبُ جُفَاءً وَأَمَّا مَا يَنفَعُ النَّاسَ فَيَمْكُثُ فِي الْأَرْضِ﴾

> "Then as for the scum, it goes to be thrown away, while that which benefits people remains on the earth."[85]

During one of the many conferences that I attended, I met a Canadian man by the name of David Forgues who accepted Islam with his wife. He was told in the beginning that the Shīʿa worship ʿAlī instead of God. This triggered him to do research about the Shīʿa, and after much sound research, he concluded that the principle of monotheism is much deeper and clearer with the Shīʿa than it is with others, so he accepted Shīʿism. This story reminds us that wisdom and intellect are more effective tools than chaos, accusations, and disruption.

Unity Between Muslims: Real or Ideal?

One of the most recurring questions concerning intra-faith harmony, unity, and proximity among the various Islamic schools of thought pertains to its objectives and feasibility. Do intra-faith unity initiatives and activities have genuine goals of proximity and understanding, or do they serve political ends only? There are two groups when it comes to this discussion.

The first group, the skeptics or pessimists, considers this activity to be a waste of time. This group is not a small group. They perceive this notion as one that is impossible to achieve. They argue that the differences are serious, and the wounds are too deep to easily be healed. Furthermore, they argue that the intra-Muslim divide is increasing daily, because sectarianism has been politicized by rivaling political powers that aim to dominate and establish hegemony over the Muslim community.

On the other hand, the optimists argue that intra-faith proximity and understanding is a viable and feasible endeavor, since history has proven that rivaling religious factions that were competing for political, social, and religious dominance were able to overcome their

---

[85] Qur'an, Sūrah al-Raʿad (13), verse 17.

differences and engage in interfaith cooperation. This is clear during the medieval era, which was riddled with bloodshed and destruction between adherents of various religious traditions, and the subsequent renaissance that gave way to create a unified platform despite their stark theological and religious differences.

Today, we witness that in some areas of North America, this interfaith understanding has led to some Christian churches hosting Jewish synagogues in their places of worship. Additionally, political, social, and cultural alliances have been established by various religious traditions, most notably the Christians and Jews in America. Thus, this level of maturity and understanding has become commonplace within various parts of the nation. The argument therefore, is that these experiences must be observed and reproduced within the Muslim communities as well.

It must be noted that in order for this intra-faith proximity to fully and genuinely materialize, some pillars must be adhered to by followers of the various Islamic schools of thought, especially the Sunnī and the Shīʿa.

First of all, scholars and the laity must initiate avenues of recognition and understanding; each learning from the mainstream and legitimate perspective of the other. This is especially important because nothing can be more destructive than basing one's understanding on polemical discussions that include suspicion, rumors, and negative stereotypes. It is noteworthy to suggest that to a large extent, Muslim communities from the various Islamic schools of thought fail to engage in positive discourse and understanding among themselves, due to a lack of approaching the genuine sources of knowledge. This is very similar to the non-Muslim skewed understanding of Islam.

One of the most significant recipes of the spike in sectarianism and leading elements of the culture of hate that has been exacerbated recently among the Muslims is the nonacademic and dogmatic approach to understanding various conflicts; and instead the dependence on false polemical discussions and accusations of each other. Thus, it is incumbent upon the scholars to understand one another from one another's reliable sources, not what is being propagated by the uneducated commoners. This is especially the case in today's age of mass communication and social media, where stereotypes and misinformation is readily available and propagated. This understanding should also not be based, for example, on the actions of some of the followers of these schools of thought who may not necessarily adhere to the primary principles of their respective school of thought.

The second pillar is based on the Qurʾanic directive to give others the benefit of the doubt in their interactions:

﴿اجْتَنِبُوا كَثِيرًا مِنَ الظَّنِّ﴾

"Avoid much suspicion."[86]

In addition to the Qurʿān, the Prophetic traditions encourage us to assume the best intentions during the course of our interactions with others.

The third factor pertains to the focus of dialogue on the large quantity of common principles, such as the Qurʾan and the acceptable Prophetic traditions among the various schools of thought. There is a famous saying among Muslim scholars that suggests that adherents cooperate with one another based on commonalities, while excusing the others in regards to differences. In other words, scholars and adherents must learn to agree to disagree when it comes to certain aspects of theology and law.

To elaborate, scholars have suggested that cooperation may exist in regards to texts that are both certain in their source and implication (*qādʿī al-ṣudūr wal dalālah*), such as those pertaining to monotheism, prophethood, the Qurʾan, acts of worship, and other similar principles. However, texts that are probable in their source and implication (*ẓannīyat al-thubūt wal dalālah*), where differences usually prevail and *ijtihad* plays a significant role, are areas in which adherents of the

[86] Qurʾan, Sūrah al-Ḥujurāt (49), verse 12.

various and differing schools of thought must be able to agree to disagree upon.

The fourth pillar is that all sides must avoid polemical discourses and derogatory remarks regarding one another. Here, we must remember the Qur'anic command and uphold it as a basis for interaction:

﴿وَقُولُوا لِلنَّاسِ حُسْنًا﴾

"And speak with one another in goodness."[87]

This includes avoiding insults of leaders and personalities who are considered sacred to the other side. It also entails avoidance of *takfīrī* discourse and language.

The fifth and final pillar pertains to the common platform for adherents of various schools of thought to cooperate on, especially in the United States. These include the various common social, political, and legal concerns, such as finding solutions to family and marriage disintegration, participation in civic and political activism, Muslim identity formation, and many others.

Impediments of Daʿwah

One of the most critical impediments to daʿwah in America is the widespread ignorance of Islam. Another is arrogance. The United States suffers from American Exceptionalism, which essentially suggests that advances in modernity, democracy, and civilization entail intellectual, military, artistic, and cultural supremacy. Therefore, some Americans reject the adoption of non-Western religion, especially Islam, which is considered a backwards and uncivilized religion. Some consider Islam to be an Arab-only phenomenon.

Many Americans are also unable to comply with Islamic religious observances, for they entail many sacrifices. Americans are used to liberal observance of religion, so joining Islam entails forgoing apparent liberties, freedoms, and comforts. As mentioned earlier, in

[87] Qur'an, Sūrah al-Baqarah (2), verse 83.

America, material lifestyle generally dominates over religious and spiritual lifestyle. Furthermore, the steady rise and effect of Islamophobia composes a great and continuous impediment to daʿwah. Factors that have exacerbated this matter are the destructive nature of the Middle East, its authoritarian regimes that are riddled with despotism and corruption, war-torn countries, the rise of refugees, and religious extremism.

Another impediment to daʿwah is the negative examples of some Muslims in the West. The model presented by Muslims through their lifestyles is not one that is often attractive to an American audience; it does not compel them to accept Islam. We find that sometimes, Muslims engage in behaviors that paint an ugly picture of Islam in the minds of non-Muslims. Furthermore, the contributions of Muslims in America are relatively modest in comparison to the contributions of other religious traditions and communities. Additionally, some Islamic centers and organizations suffer from continuous problems, including arguments and disintegration. This factor deals a great blow to effective daʿwah activities. The Qurʾan reminds us:

﴿وَلَا تَنَازَعُوا فَتَفْشَلُوا وَتَذْهَبَ رِيحُكُمْ﴾

> "And do not dispute amongst yourselves, for you will fail and lose strength."[88]

The scarcity of preachers and educators, especially in contrast to other religions, is another major impediment. During my interviews with various educators, scholars, and preachers across the United States, I found that the main reasons for this scarcity are: lack of institutions that prepare preachers, little interest by the younger generation in joining such institutions, and that daʿwah and tablīgh are exhaustive and difficult tasks that require enormous sacrifices and high diligence with low income.

Another reason for this scarcity is the modest financial resources available to the Muslim community in contrast to other religious

---

[88] Qurʾan, Sūrah al-Anfāl (8), verse 46.

communities. For example, some churches spend multi-million dollars with no effort, whereas many mosques and Islamic centers are generally in need of funds in order to even keep their doors open and continue to provide adequate programming and resources to their communities.

Banes of Tablīgh

There are a number of factors that may be expressed by the preacher or educator that destroy the fruits of tablīgh. One of the most dangerous is the epidemic of arrogance and conceit, which tends to deeply reflect on one's manners and how one interacts with others around him. Arrogance is a major impediment in the journey of spiritual and ethical nurturance.

It has been attributed to al-Shiʿbī that he stated that knowledge is three palm-widths. He went on to say that whoever possesses the first palm-width will become conceited and thinks that he has obtained all of knowledge. Once such a person receives the second palm-width, he becomes humble and realizes that he has not attained knowledge. As for the third palm-width, he states that how far it is, for no one can attain it![89]

Arrogance is a common spiritual and ethical disease among both those who are beginning their journey of tablīgh, as well as those who have established themselves for an extended period of time. The Prophet states, "He who has an atom's weight of arrogance will not enter into paradise."[90]

Imam ʿAlī narrates that Prophet Jesus turned to his disciples and asked them to grant him a need. He stood and washed the feet of his companions. They told him, we should have performed this act for you. He replied, "It is the scholar who should serve the people."[91]

One of the primary reasons for this arrogance is the excessive attention and spot light that a preacher receives from the community.

---

[89] Ibn Jamāʿa, *Tadhkiratul Sāmiʿi wal Mutakallim*, p. 65 as referenced from http://www.ahlulhadeeth.com.

[90] *Biḥār al-Anwār*, v. 70, p. 11.

[91] Al-Ḥurr al-ʿAmilī, Muḥammad ibn al-Ḥassan, *Wasāʾil al-Shīʿa*, v. 11, p. 219.

Audiences, more so the younger people, tend to give a lot of attention to preachers, especially those who are able to connect with them and speak their language. As a result, preachers are increasingly vulnerable, and allow this attention to transform into conceited behavior. This is apparent through a preacher's interaction with the community when observing regular clothing versus the religious garb. For example, a preacher may conduct himself in a manner where audiences are not able to reach or access him. One of the consequences of arrogance and conceit is that a wedge will be created between the preacher and the people, resulting in negative consequences for genuine education and inspiration.

A second related bane is social alienation. Some educators exhibit disregard for the community's needs; and they seem to alienate themselves from society. For instance, they arrive immediately before their lecture or sermon begins, and depart immediately afterwards. They may only be present when there is direct benefit to their presence. The preacher must be frequently available - like a physician, and not alienated, through contact, email, or phone.

Some preachers become rigid. Often times it is complained to me that people fear approaching a preacher or scholar for fear of angering him. To them, the preacher is easily angered, repulsive, and intolerant. However, the guidelines from religious authorities offer a clear solution.

Imam ʿAlī states, "Perhaps a man comes from an honorable lineage, however, his temperament reduces him to an estranged one; while someone comes from an unpopular lineage, but through his manners becomes attractive and well-received among the people."[92]

The Qur'an states that one reason for the success of the Prophet was his good temperament and leniency.[93]

The Prophet himself stated, "Nothing is more valuable on the scale of the Day of Judgment than good manners."[94]

---

[92] *Biḥār al-Anwār*, v. 71, p. 396.
[93] Qur'an, Sūrah Āle ʿImrān (3), verse 159.
[94] *Biḥār al-Anwār*, v. 71, p. 386.

Imam ʿAlī has narrated, "Let his (the leader's) teaching be through his manners before his speech."[95] He also mentioned, "A true scholar is the one whose actions verify one's speech."[96]

Therefore it is clear that one of the most important prerequisites for effective tablīgh is the preacher's good manners, leniency, and availability to be at the service of the community.

A third bane is the commercialization of preaching. The most dangerous deviation is to set the prime objective to be business as opposed to the service of God. The Qur'an states:

﴿اتَّبِعُوا مَن لَّا يَسْأَلُكُمْ أَجْرًا وَهُم مُّهْتَدُونَ﴾

> "Follow those who do not ask for compensation from you, and who have themselves received guidance."[97]

It has been narrated that Prophet Jesus said, "The disease of faith is the *dīnār* (money), and the physician of faith is the scholar; once you see the physician inclined towards the disease, then be suspicious of him, and be certain that he will not be a healer for others."[98]

The Prophet has stated, "The scholars are the trustees of the prophets, as long as they do not become attached to the lower life."[99]

Imam ʿAlī said: "The ornaments of this life corrupt the weak minds."[100]

Therefore, it is incumbent upon the preachers to rise above setting one's primary goal as being a material one.

A famous ḥadīth says: "God has guaranteed the sustenance of the seeker of knowledge (preacher)."[101]

Imam al-Bāqir mentioned: "Do not make us (our message) a means of income for you, otherwise God will impoverish you."[102]

---

[95] *Nahj al-Balāghah*, maxim 70.
[96] *Ghurar Al-Ḥikam*, p. 67.
[97] Qur'an, Sūrah Yāsīn (36), verse 21.
[98] Al-Ṣadūq, Muḥammad ibn ʿAlī, *al-Khiṣāl*, p. 113, ḥadīth 91.
[99] *Biḥār al-Anwār*, v. 2, p. 36.
[100] *Ghurar Al-Ḥikam*, p. 428.
[101] Al-Rayshahrī, Muḥammad, *Mīzān al-Ḥikmah*, v. 3, p. 2072.
[102] *Al-Kāfī*, v. 3, p. 406.

The Prophet said: "Woe be upon my nation of corrupt scholars; they take this knowledge as a business."[103]

Imam al-Bāqir has also said: "The Prophet cursed a person who was asked to teach them, and he asked others for money."[104]

The preacher must curb one's desire for wealth, fame, status, and leadership. It has been narrated that (the actions of) two men from the Children of Israel were mentioned before the Prophet. One of them would perform the mandatory prayers and then spend his time teaching people goodness. The other would stand in worship during the night and fast during the days. The Prophet replied that: "The virtue of the first one over the second one is like my virtue over the least among you."[105]

Thus, a preacher must be self-honored and dignified, and rise above material gains in one's journey of educating and preaching the message of God. The Qur'an states:

﴿وَمَن يَتَّقِ اللَّهَ يَجْعَل لَّهُ مَخْرَجًا وَيَرْزُقْهُ مِنْ حَيْثُ لَا يَحْتَسِبُ﴾

> "For those who are conscious of God, He will prepare a way out [for them], and He will provide for the person from sources that one could never imagine."[106]

The fourth bane is a preacher's dedication to a specific cult or group, rather than the whole community. Some preachers engage in servile flattery towards those who are wealthy or who hold certain positions in society, over other segments of society. A preacher should be available to serve everyone. People expect the preacher to be neutral and non-aligning. Thus, it is important for the educator to make sure that one is not being biased in their services and dedication to one segment of the community over another.

Finally, it is imperative that preachers and educators absolutely avoid taking advantage of individuals and communities in the name of

---

[103] *Mīzān al-Ḥikmah*, v. 6, p. 475.
[104] *Biḥār al-Anwār*, v. 2, p. 62.
[105] *Mīzān al-Ḥikmah*, v. 6, p. 474.
[106] Qur'an, Sūrah al-Ṭalāq (65), verses 2-3.

religion. The preacher is considered to be a representative of the religion, and as such, holds a great responsibility in adequately and positively representing the teachings and values of the religion. If one were to attempt to take advantage of people in the name of religion, then this would inevitably lead to the rejection of religion and its teachings.

Chapter Five: Issues Requiring Solutions

There are a number of pressing issues that preachers often face in their daʿwah and tablīgh journeys; and these require practical solutions. Based on my experiences, as well as the experiences of other scholars and preachers in the West, following are some of the problems and issues, and their proposed solutions:

The Segregation of Genders at Islamic Centers and Mosques

One of the gripping problems at Islamic centers and mosques in North America (especially the Shīʿa centers) is the struggle over the segregation of the genders.

Usually, congregations are composed of older generations, mostly immigrants from traditional societies, as well as newer second, third, and fourth generations who have been born or raised in America and consider it to be their home. In many respects, these generations hold completely different outlooks and perceptions on life, including religion and faith. Thus, one of the biggest struggles of a preacher or educator is how to reconcile between these two groups and their differing outlooks.

Proponents of segregation, many of whom lived for a considerable portion of their lives in traditional and conservative societies, find it hard to detach themselves from their long-held customs and traditions. Therefore, they consider the complete segregation of the genders as a sacred issue. They insist on erecting barriers, and within some communities, insist on completely different rooms or halls with separate entrances, where the women's only interactions with the speakers are through TV monitors. In addition, they may show resentment with inviting a female speaker to address the congregation when men are present. Strangely, some of those who believe in complete segregation have members of their own families who do not observe the ḥijāb.

As for the viewpoints of those who advocate desegregation, they argue that it is important in order to maintain a sense of organization and order, keeping unwarranted noises and distractions to a minimum. They argue that women do not pay attention to the speaker if they can not see him. This noise affects the speaker and audience and compromises the quality of the program, creating interruptions and distractions.

The second point that they suggest is that we live in a society (unlike other traditional societies) that calls for the equality of genders, one that is considered essential to civility. So the female should have an equal share in the progress and maintenance of the Islamic center and mosque. They further argue that relegating women to a secondary hall (rather than the main hall that is usually reserved for the men) will negatively impact their role as integral members of the community and society.

Another issue that proponents of desegregation present concerns the effectiveness of education. Scholars and experts argue that effective education requires firsthand and immediate interaction, dialogue, and access; and this would allow men and women to feel part and parcel of the educational experience. The establishment of a positive physical space in turn will reflect a positive mental space also. As a result, women would feel a sense of self-worth and also feel greater encouragement to contribute (financially, spiritually, and intellectually) to the cause of Islam in America.

In fact, we see that these are developing in the West. For example, the Women's Mosque of America was recently established in Los Angeles. Its aim is "to uplift the Muslim community by empowering women and girls through more direct access to Islamic scholarship and leadership opportunities. The Women's Mosque of America will provide a safe space for women to feel welcome, respected, and actively engaged within the Muslim Ummah. It will complement existing mosques, offering opportunities for women to grow, learn, and gain inspiration to spread throughout their respective communities."[1]

From personal experience, desegregation of genders in the Islamic centers and mosques results in the authentic and true appreciate of men and women. It allows them to appreciate community members like siblings or members of a family.

Based on these arguments, the preacher and educator should weigh both arguments and consider what the best approach is for the advancement and welfare of Islam and the Muslim community. This includes, first and foremost, seeking the pleasure of God, and dealing with this issue within the confines of Islamic law. In evaluating both opinions, I believe that the desegregation of genders, as long as Islamic laws are observed, is more beneficial for Islam and Muslims, allowing men and women to genuinely progress and develop.

Multiple Languages and Mentalities/Outlooks of Various Communities

This challenge pertains specifically to the American context. An Islamic center or mosque in America represents a hub for the Muslim community, not only for worshipping purposes, but it should also serve educational and social purposes, including celebrations, memorials/funerals, weddings, and other activities. Since the United States is made up of a uniquely multi-cultural society, Islamic centers are also composed of mixed backgrounds, nationalities, languages, and mentalities. Each group attempts to promote their own language and culture, sometimes forcefully. The preacher's objective then should be to unite and balance between these various factions.

Some centers that have greater financial and spatial capabilities are able to hold multiple simultaneous programs, entertaining various groups and languages. However, other centers which do not possess such capabilities are not able to entertain all of the groups.

---

[1] http://womensmosque.com/. Visited January 1, 2016.

There are two arguments here: those who insist on their own native languages argue that they enjoy listening to their own language and are not able to interact in a similar fashion with other languages, including English. Furthermore, they argue that if they do not promote their languages, they will inevitably become extinct with the new generation. Therefore, they insist on the promotion of their language.

The second group argues that the community must speak the language of the land, one that unifies all groups and brings them all together. In their view, when the groups are separated, they cluster around their own language and culture, and miss out on the main point of Islam which is unity and togetherness. As a result, this group argues that the language of the center or mosque should be strictly English. Since we live in the West, they argue, the programs must be conducted in the region's language – which is English.

As to the differing mentalities, this is one of the most difficult challenges for a preacher. Essentially, one is not able to satisfy everyone, no matter what approach a person takes. Thus, the preacher must strive to satisfy the majority, keeping in mind the impossibility of satisfying the entire community. The ḥadīth says: "Speak to the people based upon their level of cognition."[2]

From my personal experiences, I believe that the solution to the language problem is that the main programs of the Islamic centers should be conducted in English; and if needed, there should be monthly or side programs in various other languages. This way, preachers can attempt to accommodate everyone, including those who may not understand English.

The Multifaceted Clash Between the Old and New Generations

Related to what has been mentioned above, there seems to be a multifaceted and perpetual clash between those who call for progression, openness, and modernity, and those who wish to preserve old traditions and modes of expression. Preachers may frequently find

---

[2] *Biḥār al-Anwār*, v. 1, p. 106.

that their interactions with the older generation differ greatly than their interactions with the newer generation. This is also the case when it comes to interactions with converts to Islam versus those born into the religion.

We see this dynamic for example, in the month of Muḥarram. Often, there seems to be a clash when it comes to the expression of the rituals and message of ʿAshūraʾ commemorations. There are those who place extra emphasis on ritualistic expressions. They insist that ʿAshūraʾ events must emphasize the ritualistic aspects of faith; believers should have the opportunity to hear the sad events of that tragic event and mourn, weep, and engage in self-flagellation. They argue that it is the observance of these ritualistic expressions that have kept the message of ʿAshūraʾ and the name of Imam Ḥusayn alive throughout the centuries. In some centers, great time and effort is placed on preparations for these ritualistic expressions. I have personally noticed and have also been told by a number of preachers that in some centers, they witness a rise in the number of attendees of ʿAshūraʾ events during the ritualistic segments of the program, while less attendees participate during the lecture segment.

On the other hand, there are those who call for more of a focus on the message of ʿAshūraʾ through lectures, contemporary workshops, preparation for social/educational roles, and interfaith and outreach roles. They suggest that the ritualistic expressions of ʿAshūraʾ are important, but that their significance should not and does not outweigh the significance of the actual transformative and universal message of Imam Ḥusayn. Furthermore, they argue that as Muslims living in the West, it is our duty to portray Islamic values in a manner that is acceptable to a non-Muslim audience. I have personally experienced a number of newly converted Muslims who were drawn to Islam by attending the Friday prayers and other events; but were shocked to witness some of the communities who engage in excessive mourning and self-flagellation during the ʿAshūraʾ programs.

It is important for a preacher to examine this topic, which is the clash between those who insist on preserving older traditions and those who look for a more contemporary way of expressing Islam, both with an open mind and wisdom. Again, preaching Islam effectively and efficiently requires that it is done within the appropriate spatial and temporal contexts. Perhaps it may be that certain expressions are more effective in the Middle East or other parts of the world, while other expressions are more effective in the West, and in particular the United States of America. A preacher must be at the forefront of drawing and executing the most effective teaching and educational techniques at his/her disposal.

Ḥijāb and Dress Code Inside Islamic Centers

This topic presents a continuous challenge and often raises controversy and arguments in mosques and Islamic centers across the West. Various Islamic centers have introduced various measures to deal with the issue of dress code, especially ḥijāb. Some centers have completely forbidden entrance into their confines without ḥijāb; and on the other hand, some centers have absolutely allowed it. There are other centers that have restricted the observance of ḥijāb to the confines of the prayer/worship hall.

This controversy is not limited to Islamic centers and mosques, but rather extends outside the confines to other gatherings, such as conferences, banquets, weddings, and other similar events. There are those who insist that such gatherings should include a formal dress code that includes proper ḥijāb. On the other hand, there are those who oppose the implementation of such obligations and prefer to allow attendants to dress as they see fit.

An example of this occurred in the UMAA conference in 2003, whereby one of the most important and heated discussions was the permission of allowing women who were not observing the ḥijāb into the lecture halls. Opponents argued that granting permission was contradictory to Islamic law. Proponents suggested that, although not observing ḥijāb was wrong, women who were not observing ḥijāb had to be given the opportunity to attend and to listen to and benefit from their participation. They further argued that prohibiting them from such venues would not do anything but push them further away from Islamic values and strip them away of the educational and spiritual experiences that they could gain. There are many communities who hold their events at hotels in order to bypass the restricted mosque atmosphere.

In my experience, the law of God should be upheld and not compromised, and maintaining its sanctity and respect should be a core objective of preachers and Islamic organizations. Principles should not be sacrificed for the sake of modernity. In America, we find that many non-Muslim groups observe their rules and regulations, including a certain dress code, which in some cases includes head coverings – such as in Jewish, Christian, and other traditions. This is especially the case in their places of worship. Thus, in places of worship and prayer halls, ḥijāb and modest dress should be observed in order to maintain the sanctity of such places. However for public events, it may be argued that although ḥijāb is essential, it does not represent the entire core of Islam. As a result, modesty in dress and interaction should be encouraged, but we should not place absolute judgment upon people's dress code. In other words, ḥijāb is one aspect of Islamic observance, but not the only aspect. Ultimately, it is important that one prays that God bestows the inner strength to believing men and women in order to observe their commandments completely, including the ḥijāb.

Imam (Religious Scholar) and the Board/Management of Islamic Centers

In many Shīʿa and Sunnī Islamic centers across the country, frequently tensions and clashes arise between the imam and the board of directors/trustees regarding various issues. This is especially the case regarding decision-making processes.

Often the imam assumes that as the religious scholar and leader of the community, he has the absolute authority and final say concerning various decisions. However, many Islamic centers have boards of directors and/or trustees who employ a consultative and democratic procedure when it comes to making decisions concerning the center and its community. Sometimes, a clash arises between the imam and the board members.

One of the main reasons for this is because the imam in most cases, usually comes from a society that lacks democracy, and he clashes when he encounters a challenge to his decisions or a vote. On the other hand, sometimes the imam attempts to uphold a certain level of religiosity, while the board pushes back against this level of religiosity. This causes severe problems, including division, slander, verbal and sometimes even physical attacks, as in the case which transpired in Denver, Colorado, in which an Islamic center was confiscated and sold as a result of domestic disputes among the members.

Sometimes, the division occurs between board members themselves. Some center boards are composed of members who often possess different and occasionally contradicting lifestyles and outlooks. There are those who are religiously observant, while others may be non-observant. Some express exclusive behavior, while their counterparts are inclusive and tolerant; some emphasize Islamic values while others emphasize culture; some are open-minded, while others are narrow-minded; some focus on communal objectives, while others participate purely for personal objectives.

Other types of conflicts pertain to the differences between religious injunctions according to various religious authorities, and the divisions that they may cause. For example, a recurring problem is that of the confirmation for the beginning and end of the lunar months, especially the month of Ramaḍān and Shawwāl (ʿĪd). It may be observed that within some communities and centers, three consecutive days have been designated as the beginning of the month! This problem creates confusion and disenchantment among communities and its members.

The religion of Islam and specifically, the teachings of the Ahlulbayt emphasize the role of cohesiveness and cooperation, especially among religious leaders and educators who invite people to path of God. We find that many educators do their best to unify and foster the spirit of togetherness, while others unfortunately, intentionally attempt to cause division and problems. The result of this is that the community in turn holds religion accountable. This is because educators are perceived by community members to be the representatives of the religion. The actions of preachers and educators are not analyzed as actions of individuals, but reflective of religion as a whole.

These types of conflicts frequently sidetrack educators and communities from their main goal, which is the propagation of Islam.

Collection, Use, and Distribution of Religious Dues

To a large extent, Islamic centers in America base their financial sources on zakāt and khums as the main sources of funding. In fact, we find that the building, maintenance, and propagation of mosques and Islamic centers constitute one of the most significant portions for the distribution and use of religious dues according to Islamic law. However, one of the biggest problems that preachers and Islamic centers across the nation face pertains to the collection, use, and distribution of these religious dues.

One of the major challenges concerning this problem is the misappropriation of zakāt and khums. The underlying problem is a lack of transparency on part of some religious preachers and/or centers in how these funds are acquired, and more importantly, how they are used and spent. Often we find complaints by various community members regarding this topic. Many Islamic centers continue to face financial challenges, and in some cases, this is due to the misuse of religious dues.

Lack of Attempts at and Resources for Daʿwah and Tablīgh

As mentioned in earlier sections of this work, Islamic centers in general are not appropriately equipped for daʿwah and tablīgh - especially daʿwah. Effective daʿwah requires certain capacities, methods, and approaches. Among them, daʿwah requires vibrant, dynamic preachers, especially those who are able to express themselves in multiple languages, such as English, Spanish, and other relevant languages. Various studies, reports, and interviews have verified that there is a great lack in the number of preachers in America, especially those who may be considered effective for successful daʿwah activities. Additionally, many imams leading in local mosques and even some preachers do not possess the adequate religious training to answer various theological and legal questions, nor are they able to provide other important services.

Furthermore, there is a lack of adequate and relevant resources for daʿwah and tablīgh. For example, we find that there is a plethora of books and articles that have been published online, but many of these lack relevant content, or the translations from their original languages are deficient. Further, there is a severe lack in relevant multimedia resources. For example, there exist dozens of Islamic satellite channels on the air, but the vast majority of them are unresponsive to the various intellectual, religious, and social needs of society. We find that some of these channels promote completely irrelevant issues, while others promote negative issues such as sectarianism. Within the Shīʿa community, this problem is exacerbated.

Finally, most centers lack programs that are specifically catered for converts; and In fact, the environment is not even conducive to attracting converts. This is either because these centers do not seem to feel the need to promote daʿwah activities and attract converts; or because of ethnic, racial, cultural, or language barriers which all prevent people from wanting to come and investigate and learn about Islam.

It is essential for preachers to understand the significance of focusing on both daʿwah and tablīgh initiatives and activities. These include promoting and participating in various programs that are specially catered for non-Muslims, such as interfaith programs; or with other schools of thought within Islam, such as intra-faith programs; as well as specific programs that aid converts in adapting to their new lives and communities during and after their journeys of embracing Islam.

Furthermore, Islamic centers and mosques need to focus on producing and maintaining adequate daʿwah and tablīgh resources in the forms of books, articles, pamphlets, websites, and audio/video material. Many non-Muslims, converts, as well as the Muslim community members rely heavily on these resources to enhance their understanding of Islam and find solutions for challenges that they face in their day-to-day lives in the West.

Chapter Six: Conclusion

In the introduction of this work, I proposed that the current and future state of daʿwah and tablīgh in the West is that successful daʿwah and tablīgh will continue to pose a formidable challenge for the Western Muslim community, but will certainly be promising if the aforementioned points are placed at the forefront of the various daʿwah and tablīgh initiatives and activities in America. The success or lack of it will largely depend on the American Muslim community's willingness to engage with the most pressing issues - those pertaining to educating the general public about Islam, as well as educating the Muslim community.

Current reports suggest that Islam is the fastest growing religion in the world, and that it will continue to be so for the next four decades.[1] Although much of the growth of the religion is due to the rise in numbers of Muslims in the Middle East, Africa, and Southeast Asia, the number of Muslims in the West is similarly growing at a rapid pace. In the United States of America, reports suggest that by 2050, Islam will be the second largest religion after Christianity.[2] With the rapid increase in the number of Muslims and the growth of Islam in America, it is essential to examine the role of preaching and educating both non-Muslims as well as Muslims about Islam. This is referred to in Arabic as daʿwah and tablīgh, respectively.

The significance, objectives, and methods of daʿwah and tablīgh, as well as the role and characteristics of preachers and educators have been analyzed extensively in this work.

The following are some brief points to summarize our discussion:

---

[1] http://www.pewforum.org/2015/04/02/religious-projections-2010-2050/. Visited January 1, 2016.
[2] Ibid.

a. As far as Islam is concerned, the most sanctified task that one can undertake is to communicate the message that was received by the messengers from God to the people. Numerous traditions emphasize that this strenuous task is one that holds boundless rewards. This effort culminates in what is known in the Islamic tradition as daʿwah and tablīgh. In this work, daʿwah referred to the education and invitation of non-Muslims to Islam, while tablīgh referred to the education of Muslims about their religious tradition. The objectives of this task then, are to enable human beings to reach the status of human perfection and be suitable to be God's vicegerents on this earth.

   As mentioned, there are three main components to daʿwah and tablīgh: the first is the content of the message that is being propagated; the second is the character of the preacher; and the third is the character of the invitee. The most important feature of daʿwah and tablīgh in Islam is that which is based on wisdom, good advice, and harmonious debate. This concept in fact, is not confined to Islam, but also occupies a fundamental place in other religious traditions as well. This is true in the case of Christianity for instance, and the effort and resources allocated to evangelism.

b. The case study for this book is focused on the United States. In America, religion is a very important part in shaping American identity. Many Americans believe in the existence of a higher power and engage in ritualistic expressions of their faith. We can say that in terms of religious identity, America is the most religiously diverse nation in the world. From the beginning, America was established on principles of freedom of religion and expression. Reports indicate that American society is generally non-dogmatic. Among the most important social tendencies of Americans is that they hold strong work ethic, they are action oriented, they are competitive, they engage in extensive philanthropy and they express individualism and materialism, which is exhibited in its strongest and most profound terms. This is clearly the case in regards to what is popularly known as pursuing the "American Dream."

c. The origin of Islam in America can be traced back to well over one thousand years ago. Thousands of Muslims were brought to the American shores through the sixteenth century slave trade and subsequent migrations occurred throughout recent centuries. Muslim presence in contemporary America is composed mainly of recent immigrants, converts, and second, third, and fourth generation Muslims, the majority of which are recent immigrants.

Among these Muslims, the vast majority are Sunnī, and there exists a sizable Shīʿa minority also, in addition to Ṣufīs and others. The Shīʿa make up about one-fifth of the Muslim population in America. There currently exists Shīʿa Islamic centers in almost all of the states, with the largest concentrations in California, Michigan, New York, Illinois, Texas, and others.

Muslims in America endure many challenges, as well as benefit from many opportunities; and they are not a monolith. Rather, the Muslim community is highly diverse.

In general, Muslims can be categorized into: assimilationists (those who tend to fully immerse themselves into society); isolationists (those who tend to distance themselves from all forms of participation in public life); and integrationists (those who tend to engage in American culture while maintaining their distinct identities).

While Islam is the fastest growing religion in America, the issues surrounding conversion to Islam are not always without tension and problems. Converts face many challenges in their experiences with cultural Islam. While America is the most religiously diverse nation, unfortunately Islam continues to be one of the most misunderstood religions. Reports suggest that one in two Americans holds unfavorable views of Islam and Muslims. The rise of Islamophobia is the Muslims' biggest challenge today in America. Islamophobia stems from various groups, including right-wing media, religious groups, and anti-Islam bigots and pundits.

d. Despite the existence of over two thousand Islamic centers and mosques in America, it seems that the vast majority cater to the immigrant Muslim community. Many are highly ethnocentric, and suffer from a lack of English speaking preachers and educators. Most Islamic centers are not adequately equipped for Islamic daʿwah activities. Only a small number of Islamic centers focus their efforts on daʿwah and widen their scope to include converts and non-Muslim communities in their activities.

Although many preachers may have been educated in the field of theoretical daʿwah, however they seem to be poorly equipped when it comes to practical daʿwah.

Due to factors such as the existence of freedom of religion (guaranteed by the United States Constitution), federal tax-exempt status for non-profit religious organizations, the accessibility of the means of religious propagation (such as the Internet, social media, and TV/radio channels), the potential for daʿwah in the North America is unique and incomparable to any other place in the world.

There are a number of mediums and approaches to effective daʿwah in America; among them are: (1) the oral communication of the message through lectures, classes, discussions, sermons; (2) literature through blogs, books, articles, social media; (3) artistic expressions through art and poetry; and (4) family and youth activities such as camps and retreats.

Also important is the content of daʿwah, areas of which include: theological discussions; contemporary issues (such as pluralism, tolerance, religious extremism); social issues (marriage and family); and ethical issues (forgiveness, compassion, charity). Among the most important areas of tablīgh are: the role of Islam and Muslims in The West; the significance of integration into American society; and ethical and moral issues (parenting, safeguarding of family, inter-gender relations, ethical business transactions).

Since the character of a preacher plays a major role in the delivery of the message to the hearts and minds of the people, their moral characteristics are of prime importance. Among the most significant characteristics are: the spiritual refinement of oneself, dedication, earnestness, perseverance, genuine care and compassion.

Among the most important intellectual characteristics of a preacher are: proficiency of scholarship, and commitment to the continuity of knowledge. Finally, among the most important practical characteristics of a preacher are: oratory skills, and possession of adequate awareness of the needs and demographics within one's audience.

One of the greatest types of social relationships in the United States is developed through interfaith dialogue and activities. The objective of these activities is not to convert one another, but to understand each other. American Muslims have significantly benefited from their interfaith engagements and relationships. Among the most important fruits of interfaith relations is the non-Muslim voices that come to the defense of Muslims during many anti-Islamic incidents.

Muslims in America have also been able to establish amicable intra-faith relations, among the Sunnī and Shīʿa, based on mutual respect and cooperation. Nonetheless, the legacy that contemporary sectarianism try to push continues to adversely influence some Muslims on both sides.

There are a number of impediments to daʿwah and tablīgh activities in America. Among the most significant are: widespread ignorance of Islam; arrogance due to American exceptionalism; the negative example that some Muslims present in the West; the scarcity of qualified preachers and educators; and the lack of resources and will power for such activities.

There are many outstanding challenges that face the Muslim communities. In the forefront are: the multifaceted clash between old and new generations; multiple languages and diverse mentalities; dress code and segregation of genders at Islamic centers; and the collection and use of religious dues.

The Future of Daʿwah and Tablīgh in the West

Islam has very deep historical roots in North America. However today, Islamic ideology, culture, and customs remain largely alien to American society. This is because essentially, the United States of America was built on religious foundations that were imported from Europe, which was heavily Christian. Many people today consider the United States as first and foremost a Judeo-Christian nation. Despite the existence of some studies that suggest that Islam will be the second largest religion in America in a few decades, yet careful and farsighted indications seem to suggest that Islam will remain largely confined to immigrant circles, as well as the African-American community, and that Islam will continue to remain misunderstood for the foreseeable future.

There are undeniable factors that mitigate the spread of an acceptable Islam in America. One of the most significant of these is the profound sense of race and ethnic divisions, especially within the Muslim communities. Although the Muslim community is one of the most diverse communities, yet it largely remains ethnocentric and isolated from other communities. Furthermore, Americans are deeply affected by the media, and current negative media reports and portrayals of Islam and Muslims, as well as ongoing deadly conflicts in the Muslim world, have a tremendous effect on Americans and their perceptions of Islam.

However, if Muslims are serious about changing unfavorable perceptions and views about Islam and allowing it to prosper in the West, then two areas must be focused on. The first is the Muslim community's extensive integration into society: Muslims must put a human face to their religion. They must be able to integrate into all sectors of society so as to be visible and recognizable. This means that Muslims must engage in and adopt every profession - from plumbers to teachers, to physicians, to lawyers, to movie directors, to actors, to financial advisors, to astronauts, and policy makers.

The second area of focus is that Muslims must seriously engage in philanthropy and community service work that extends outside the boundaries of their own religious traditions. This includes the establishment of hospitals, clinics, soup kitchens, charities, and other similar ventures. Despite the existence of thousands of Muslim physicians, there is not a single hospital that has been established by the Muslims. On the other hand, other religious traditions, such as Christianity, have built hundreds of hospitals across America. Not only have Christians been able to successfully establish such organizations, but they have even been able to adopt methods and practices that have allowed their churches and organizations to prosper, such as their management in a businesslike and effective manner. If Muslims want to make a difference, they must realize that current models of management in the Islamic centers, mosques, schools, and other organizations have become largely outdated, and new and contemporary methods of daʿwah are extremely essential today.

Closing Prayer

I conclude this work, *An American Muslim Preacher: Nuances of Islam in the West* with a supplication which was taught by the fourth successor of the Prophet of Islām, named ʿAlī the son of Ḥusayn - who carries the honorific title of *The Ornament of the Worshippers.*

In his passionate appeal to the Most High, he makes the following prayer in his *Whispered Prayer of the Obedient towards God.*

In the Name of God, the All-Merciful, the All-Compassionate

O God, inspire us to obey You;
And turn us away from disobeying You;
Make it easy for us to reach the seeking
of Your good pleasure which we wish;
Set us down in the midst of Your Gardens;
Dispel from our insights the clouds of misgiving;
Uncover from our hearts the wrappings of doubt and the veil;
Make falsehood vanish from our innermost minds,
And fix the truth in our secret thoughts,
For doubts and opinions fertilize temptations,
And muddy the purity of gifts and kindnesses!

O God, carry us in the ships of Your deliverance;
Give us to enjoy the pleasure of whispered prayer to You;
Make us drink at the pools of Your love;
Let us taste the sweetness of Your affection and nearness;
Allow us to struggle in Your way;

Preoccupy us with obeying You;
And purify our intentions in devoting works to You,
For we exist through You and belong to You,
And we have no one to mediate with You other than You!

My God, place me among the chosen, the good.
Join me to the righteous, the pious;
The first to reach generous gifts;
The swift to come upon good things,
The workers of the abiding acts of righteousness,
The strivers after elevated degrees!
You are powerful over everything and disposed to respond!
By Your mercy,
O Most Merciful of the merciful!

Bibliography

"A Portrait of Jewish Americans." Pew Research Centers Religion Public Life Project RSS. September 30, 2013. Accessed July 26, 2015. http://www.pewforum.org/2013/10/01/jewish-american-beliefs-attitudes-culture-survey/.

"A Portrait of Muslim Americans." Pew Research Center for the People and the Press RSS. August 29, 2011. Accessed July 26, 2015. http://www.people-press.org/2011/08/30/a-portrait-of-muslim-americans/.

Abdullah, Aslam, and Gasser Hathout. *The American Muslim Identity: Speaking for Ourselves*. Los Angeles, CA: Multimedia Vera International, 2003.

"About the Office of Faith-based and Neighborhood Partnerships." The White House. Accessed July 26, 2015. https://www.whitehouse.gov/administration/eop/ofbnp/about.

Abu Nuʿaym Al-Isfahani, Aḥmad Ibn ʿAbdullah. *Hilyat Al-Awliyāʾ Wa Tabaqat Al-Asfiyāʾ* Beirut: Dar Al-Kutub Al-Ilmiyyah.

Abul Aynayn Badran, Badran. *Al-Ilaqat Al-Ijtimaʾiyyah Bayn Al-Muslimin Wa Ghayr Al-Muslimin Fi Al-Shariʿah Al-Islamiyyah Wal Yahudiyyah Wal Masihiyyah Wal Qanun*. Beirut: Dar Al-Nahdhah Al-Arabiyyah, 1984.

Ahmed, Akbar S. *Journey into America: The Challenge of Islam*. Washington, D.C.: Brookings Institution Press, 2010.

Al-Afrīqī, Muḥammad Ibn Mukram Ibn Manẓur. *Lisān Al-ʿArab*. Beirut: Dar Sadir, 2010.

Al-Bajari, Jafar. *Al-Tabligh: Manahijuhu Wa Asalibuhu*. Qum: Al-Markaz Al-Alami Lil Dirasat Al-Islamiyyah, 2007.

Al-Jawharī, Isma'īl Ibn Hammad. *Al-Ṣiḥāḥ*. Beirut: Dar Al-Ilm Lil Malayin, 1987.

Al-Kulaynī, Muḥammad Ibn Ya'qūb. *Al-Kāfī*. Beirut: Dar Al-Ta'aruf, 1992.

Al-Majlisī, Muḥammad Bāqir. *Biḥār Al-Anwār*. Beirut: Dar Ihya' Al-Turath, 1983.

Al-Muttaqī Al-Hindī, 'Alī Ibn Abd Al-Malik. *Kanz Al-'Ummāl*. Cairo: Muassassat Al-Risalah, 1981.

Al-Māzandarānī, Muḥammad Ṣaliḥ. *Sharḥ Uṣūl Al-Kāfī*. Edited by Ali 'Ashur. Beirut: Muassassat Al-Tarikh Al-Arabi, 2008.

Al-Qardhawi, Yusuf. *Ghayr Al-Muslimin Fil Mujtama Al-Islami*. Beirut: Muassassat Al-Risalah, 1994.

Al-Qazwini, Sayed Moustafa. *Tajribatī Fil Gharb*. Beirut: Dar Al-Uloum, 2011.

Al-Rayshahrī, Muḥammad. *Mīzān Al-Ḥikmah*. Qum: Dar Al-Hadith, 1995.

Al-Raysuni, Ahmad. *Imam Al-Shatibi's Theory of the Higher Objectives and Intents of Islamic Law*. London: International Institute of Islamic Thought, 2005.

Al-Rāghib Al-Isfahānī, Ḥusayn. *Al-Mufradāt Fī Gharīb Al-Qur'an*. Beirut: Dar Al-Ma'rifah.

Al-Sharīf Al-Raḍhī, Muḥammad Ibn Ḥusayn. *Nahj al-Balāghah*. Edited by Subhi Al-Salih. Beirut: Dar Al-Kitab Al-Lubnani, 2004.

Al-Zuhayli, Wahbah. *Al-Ilaqat Al-Duwaliyyah Fil Islam*. Beirut: Muassassat Al-Risalah, 1981.

Al-Āmidī, 'Abd Al-Wahid. *Ghurar Al-Ḥikam*. Beirut: Muassassat Al-Alami, 2002.

Al-Ḥalabī, 'Alī Ibn Burhan Al-Din. *Al-Sīrah Al-Ḥalabiyyah*. Damascus: Dar Al-Nawadir, 2013.

Al-Ḥurr Al-ʿAmilī, Muḥammad Ibn Al-Ḥassan. *Wasāʾil Al-Shīʿa.* Beirut: Aalulbayt Li Ihya' Al-Turath, 1993.

Al-Ṣadūq, Muḥammad Ibn ʿAlī. *Al-Amālī.* Beirut: Muassassat Al-A'lami, 2009.

Al-Ṣadūq, Muḥammad Ibn ʿAlī. *Kitab Al-Khiṣāl.* Qum: Jama'at Al-Mudarrisin, 1982.

Al-Ṭabāʾtabāʾī, Sayyid Muḥammad Ḥusayn. *Al-Mīzān Fī Tafsīr Al-Qurʾan.* Beirut: Dar Ihya' Al-Turath, 2006.

Al-Ṭūsī, Muḥammad Ibn Ḥasan. *Al-Tibyān Fi Tafsīr Al-Qurʾan.* Beirut: Dar Ihya' Al-Turath.

Ali, Wajahat. *Fear, Inc.: The Roots of the Islamophobia Network in America.* Center for American Progress, 2011.

"America's Changing Religious Landscape." Pew Research Centers Religion Public Life Project RSS. May 11, 2015. Accessed July 26, 2015. http://www.pewforum.org/2015/05/12/americas-changing-religious-landscape/.

Ardestani, Ahmad Sadeqdi. *Raveshhaye Tabligh Wa Sukhanrani.* Qum: Daftare Tablighate Islami, 2011.

Babazadeh, Ali Akbar. *Shivehaye Taʿlim Wa Tabligh.* Qum: Intisharate Danesh Va Adab, 2003.

Bellah, Robert N. "Civil Religion in America." *Daedalus*, no. 96 (1967): 1-21.

Berger, J. M., and Jonathan Morgan. "The ISIS Twitter Census." Brookings Center for Middle East Policy. March 1, 2015. Accessed July 27, 2015.
http://www.brookings.edu/~/media/research/files/papers/2015/03/isis-twitter-census-berger-morgan/isis_twitter_census_berger_morgan.pdf.

"Catholic Charities USA 2013 Annual Survey." Scribd. Accessed July 27, 2015. http://www.scribd.com/doc/239473494/2013-Annual-Survey-Overview.

"Converts to Islam." Pew Research Center RSS. July 20, 2007. Accessed July 26, 2015. http://www.pewresearch.org/daily-number/converts-to-Islam/.

Converts to Islam. Qum: Ansariyan Publications, 2005.

Dirks, Jerald. *The Abrahamic Faiths: Judaism, Christianity, and Islam: Similarities and Contrasts.* Beltsville, MD: Amana Publications, 2004.

Dirks, Jerald. *Muslims in American History: A Forgotten Legacy.* Beltsville, Md.: Amana Publications, 2006.

Eck, Diana L. *A New Religious America: How A "Christian Country" Has Now Become The World's Most Religiously Diverse Nation.* San Francisco: HarperSanFrancisco, 2001.

Eckersley, Richard. "Is Modern Western Culture a Health Hazard?" *International Journal of Epidemiology* 35, no. 2 (2005): 252-58. Accessed July 27, 2015.
http://ije.oxfordjournals.org/content/35/2/252.full.

Ehrman, Bart D. *Jesus, Interrupted: Revealing the Hidden Contradictions in the Bible (and Why We Don't Know About Them).* New York, NY: HarperOne, 2009.

Fadhlallāh, Sayyid Muḥammad Husayn. *Uslub Al-Da'wah Fil Qur'an.* 6th ed. Beirut: Dar Al-Malak, 1997.

Fadl, Khaled. *The Great Theft: Wrestling Islam From The Extremists.* New York, NY: HarperSanFrancisco, 2005.

Fairūzābādī, Majd Ud-Dīn. *Al-Qāmūs Al-Muḥīṭ.* Beirut: Muassassat Al-Risalah, 2005.

"Faith in Flux." Pew Research Centers Religion Public Life Project RSS. April 26, 2009. Accessed July 26, 2015.
http://www.pewforum.org/2009/04/27/faith-in-flux/.

Fool, Katherine. "20 Ways Americans Are Blowing Their Money." USA Today. March 24, 2014. Accessed July 26, 2015.
http://www.usatoday.com/story/money/personalfinance/2014/03/24/20-ways-we-blow-our-money/6826633/.

Ghallūsh, Aḥmad. *Al-Daʿwah Al-Islamiyyah: Usūluhā Wa Wasāʾiluhā.* Beirut: Dar Al-Kitab Al-Lubnani, 1987.

"Growing Concern about Rise of Islamic Extremism at Home and Abroad." Pew Research Center for the People and the Press RSS. September 10, 2014. Accessed July 26, 2015. http://www.people-press.org/2014/09/10/growing-concern-about-rise-of-Islamic-extremism-at-home-and-abroad/.

Hathout, Hassan. *Reading the Muslim Mind.* Plainfield, IN: American Trust Publications, 1995.

Hathout, Maher. *Jihad vs. Terrorism.* Edited by Samer Hathout. Los Angeles, CA: Multimedia Vera International, 2002.

Hathout, Maher, Uzma Jamil, Gasser Hathout, and Nayyer Ali. *In Pursuit of Justice: The Jurisprudence of Human Rights in Islam.* Los Angeles, CA: Muslim Public Affairs Council, 2006.

"Humanitarian Services." Humanitarian Services. Accessed July 26, 2015. http://www.ldsphilanthropies.org/humanitarian-services.html.

Hāshim, Aḥmad 'Umar. *Al-Daʿwah Al-Islamiyyah: Manhajuhā Wa Maʿālimuhā.* Cairo: Dar Gharib.

Ibn Abī Shaybah, Abu Bakr. *Al-Muṣannaf.* Riyadh: Maktabat Al-Rushd, 1988.

Ibn Ashur, Muḥammad Al-Tahir. *Ibn Ashur: Treatise on Maqāṣid Al-Shariʿah.* Herndon, VA: International Institute of Islamic Thought, 2006.

Ibn Jamāʿa. *Tadhkiratul Sāmiʿi Wal Mutakallim.* 3rd ed. Beirut: Dar Al-Basha'ir Al-Islamiyyah, 2012.

Ibn Ḥanbal, Aḥmad. *Musnad Aḥmad Ibn Ḥanbal.* Edited by Shuʿayb Al-Arnaʿud. Beirut: Muassassat Al-Risalah, 1995.

"Islamic Daʿwa Center: Milwaukee's Central Mosque." RSS. Accessed July 26, 2015. http://www.dawahcenter.org/.

"Islamic Daʿwah Center." Islamic Daʿwah Center. Accessed July 26,

2015. http://www.islamicdawahcenter.org/.

Kaleem, Jaweed. "More Than Half Of Americans Have Unfavorable View Of Islam, Poll Finds." The Huffington Post. Accessed July 26, 2015. http://www.huffingtonpost.com/2015/04/10/americans-islam-poll_n_7036574.html.

Khan, M. A. Muqtedar, ed. *American Journal of Islamic Social Sciences* 22, no. 3, 2005.

"LADO - A Latino/Hispanic Muslim Organization That Promotes Islam." Accessed July 26, 2015. http://www.latinodawah.org.

Legislating Fear: Islamophobia and Its Impact on the United States. Washington, DC: Council on American-Islamic Relations, 2013.

Mahmasani, Subhi. *Al-Qanun Wal Ilaqat Al-Duwaliyyah Fil Islam.* 2nd ed. Beirut: Dar Al-Ilm Lil Malayin, 1982.

Morrow, John A. *The Covenants of the Prophet Muḥammad with the Christians of the World.* Angelico Press, 2013.

"Muslims." Pew Research Centers Religion Public Life Project RSS. April 2, 2015. Accessed July 26, 2015. http://www.pewforum.org/2015/04/02/muslims/.

Nasr, Seyyed Hossein. *The Garden of Truth: The Vision and Promise of Sufism, Islam's Mystical Tradition.* New York: HarperOne, 2007.

Nasr, Seyyed Vali Reza. *The Shia Revival: How Conflicts within Islam Will Shape the Future.* New York: Norton, 2006.

"Number of U.S. Mosques up 74% since 2000." USATODAY.COM. Accessed July 26, 2015. http://usatoday30.usatoday.com/news/religion/story/2012-02-29/Islamic-worship-growth-us/53298792/1.

Rahbar, Muḥammad Taqi. *Pijoshi Dar Bareye Tabligh.* Qum: Muassese Bustane Kitab, 2012.

Rahman, Jamal. *Spiritual Gems of Islam: Insights & Practices from the Qur'an, Hadith, Rumi & Muslim Teaching Stories to Enlighten the Heart*

& Mind. Woodstock, VT: SkyLight Paths Pub., 2013.

"Religion in the News: Islam Was No. 1 Topic in 2010." Pew Research Centers Religion Public Life Project RSS. February 23, 2011. Accessed July 26, 2015. http://www.pewforum.org/2011/02/24/religion-in-the-news-Islam-was-no-1-topic-in-2010/.

Shafiq, Muḥammad, and Mohammed Abu-Nimer. *Interfaith Dialogue: A Guide for Muslims.* Herndon, VA: International Institute of Islamic Thought, 2007.

Shihab, Alwi, and Ralph B. Brown. *Examining Islam in the West: Addressing Accusations and Correcting Misconceptions.* Jakarta: Gramedia Pustaka Utama, 2004.

Takim, Liyakatali. *Shi'ism in America.* New York: New York University Press, 2009.

"The Almanac of American Philanthropy | The Philanthropy Roundtable." Accessed July 26, 2015. http://www.philanthropyroundtable.org/almanac.

"The Bill of Rights: A Transcription." National Archives and Records Administration. Accessed July 26, 2015. http://www.archives.gov/exhibits/charters/bill_of_rights_transcript.html.

"The Future of World Religions: Population Growth Projections, 2010-2050." Pew Research Centers Religion Public Life Project RSS. April 2, 2015. Accessed July 26, 2015. http://www.pewforum.org/2015/04/02/religious-projections-2010-2050/.

"The Future of the Global Muslim Population." Pew Research Centers Religion Public Life Project RSS. January 26, 2011. Accessed July 26, 2015. http://www.pewforum.org/2011/01/27/the-future-of-the-global-muslim-population/#the-americas.

The Holy Qur'an.

"The Women's Mosque of America." Accessed July 26, 2015.

http://womensmosque.com/.

Tripp, Charles. *A History of Iraq*. 3rd ed. Cambridge: Cambridge University Press, 2007.

"U.S. Dominates List of World's 500 Most Influential Muslims" Washington Post. November 28, 2012. Accessed July 26, 2015. http://www.washingtonpost.com/national/on-faith/us-dominates-list-of-worlds500-most-influential-muslims/2012/11/28/27187f62-3999-11e2-9258-ac7c78d5c680_story.html.

U.S. Religious Landscape Survey, 2008. Washington, D.C.: Pew Research Center, 2008.

"USMCO Members." US Council of Muslim Organizations. Accessed July 26, 2015. http://www.uscmo.org/members/.

"United States Census Bureau." Computer and Internet Use Main. Accessed July 26, 2015. http://www.census.gov/hhes/computer/.

"Use It and Lose It: The Outsize Effect of U.S. Consumption on the Environment." Scientific American Global RSS. Accessed July 26, 2015. http://www.scientificamerican.com/article/american-consumption-habits/.

Walbridge, Linda S. *Without Forgetting the Imam: Lebanese Shiʿism in an American Community*. Detroit, MI: Wayne State University Press, 1997.

Younis, Ahmed. *American Muslims: Voir Dire*. Los Angeles, CA: Multimedia Vera International, 2002.

Yusuf, Mahmoud Abd Al-Fattah. *Min Ahkam Al-Harb Fi Al-Shariʿah Al-Islamiyyah Wal Qanun*. Cairo: Dar Al-Fikr Al-Arabi.

Zamani, Muḥammad Hasan. *Taharat Wa Najasat Ahle Kitab Wa Mushrikan Dar Fiqhe Islami*. Qum: Markaze Intisharate Daftare Tablighate Islami, 1999.

"Al Ajwah Islamic Dawah Learning Center." Accessed July 26, 2015. http://al-ajwah.org/.

ʻAbdulʿazīz, Jumʿah Amīn. *Al-Daʿwah: Qawaʻid Wa Usūl.* 4th ed. Cairo: Dar Al-Da'wah, 1999.

Ḥasan, Muḥammad Amīn. *Khaṣāʾiṣ Al-Daʿwah Al-Islamiyyah.* Dar Al-Thaqafah, 2000.

Glossary of Terms

Aḥādīth: Plural of *ḥadīth.* Refers to a statement or saying of Prophet Muḥammad, his daughter Fāṭimah al-Zahrā᾽, or one of the twelve designated successors of the Prophet.

Ahl al-Kitāb: Lit. People of the Book – an honorific title reserved for Jews, Christians and other previous religions which were given a Divinely-sent scripture.

Ahlulbayt: Lit. People of the House – a designation for the members of the family of Prophet Muḥammad and includes his daughter, Fāṭima al-Zahrā᾽, her husband ʿAlī ibn Abī Ṭālib and their two sons, al-Ḥasan and al-Ḥusayn.

ʿAlawī: A religious sect living mainly in Syria and Turkey that originated from Shia Islam, but separated from other Shia groups in the ninth and tenth centuries.

Banī Isrā᾽īl: Lit. Tribes of Israel – refers to the offspring of Prophet Jacob who formed the twelve tribes of Israel – one from each of his sons.

Daʿwah: The process of educating and inviting non-Muslims to knowledge and awareness of Islam.

Druze: A religious sect originating among Muslims and centered mainly in Lebanon and Syria.

Ḥadīth: A statement or saying of Prophet Muḥammad or one of his twelve designated successors – see *aḥādīth (pl).*

Ḥajj: The major pilgrimage to Mecca and the surrounding areas, it takes place once a year during the twelfth lunar month which is called *Dhu al-Ḥijjah.*

Ḥijāb: Commonly used to refer to the specific form of modest dress which Muslim women are obligated to wear while in the presence of men whom they are not related to via marriage or direct blood relation.

Imām: Lit. leader, this word carries with it various connotations and is used for the prayer leader of a mosque; a spiritual guide within the Muslim community; and also a Divinely-appointed guide for humanity – such as Prophet Abraham and also the twelve Divinely-appointed successors of Prophet Muḥammad.

Imam ʿAlī: Full name is ʿAlī ibn Abī Ṭālib – he is the first of the twelve Imāms or Divinely-appointed successors of Prophet Muḥammad.

Imam al-Bāqir: Full name is Muḥammad ibn ʿAlī – he is the fifth of the twelve Imāms or Divinely-appointed successors of Prophet Muḥammad.

Imam al-Ḥasan: Full name is al-Ḥasan ibn ʿAlī – he is the second of the twelve Imāms or Divinely-appointed successors of Prophet Muḥammad.

Imam al-Ḥusayn: Full name is al-Ḥusayn ibn ʿAlī – he is the third of the twelve Imāms or Divinely-appointed successors of Prophet Muḥammad.

Imam al-Riḍā: Full name is ʿAlī ibn Mūsā – he is the eighth of the twelve Imāms or Divinely-appointed successors of Prophet Muḥammad.

Imam as-Ṣādiq: Full name is Jaʿfar ibn Muḥammad – he is the sixth of the twelve Imāms or Divinely-appointed successors of Prophet Muḥammad.

Interfaith: The process of dialogue and discussion with people from other faiths to come to common agreements and understandings.

Intra-Faith: The process of dialogue and discussion with people from the same faith to come to common agreements and understandings.

Jihād: A term which has multiple meanings, it literally means "struggle" and can denote the inner struggle against one's passions, whims and desires and also refers to a struggle to protect and safeguard one's home and possessions from outside aggression.

Khums: An Islamic tax mentioned in the Qur'ān which is levied at the rate of 20% of one's net savings.

People of the Book: See *Ahl al-Kitāb.*

Shī'a: The full name being the Shī'a of 'Alī, this title is used for those who believe that after the demise of Prophet Muḥammad, 'Alī was the first successor – both in temporal and spiritual matters – it literally means 'a follower'. The Shī'a are followers of Islam as taught by Prophet Muḥammad, however believe that the true path of knowledge of Islam and its teachings cannot be gained except through following the teachings imparted by 'Alī and his eleven descendants.

Sufism: A branch of Islam focused on mysticism.

Sunnī: A title which denotes the majority of the followers of Islām, and those who follow the *sunnah* or tradition and teachings of Prophet Muḥammad.

Tablīgh: The process of preaching to and teaching Islam.

Takfīrī: An accusation which one Muslim levels against another Muslim (or an adherent of another Abrahimic faith) of apostasy; the accusation itself is called *takfīr* and is derived from the word *kāfir* (unbeliever). This term has taken on a sectarian slur in recent years.

Tawrāt: The Torah – the Divine book given to Prophet Moses.

'Umrah: The Minor Pilgrimage performed in Mecca outside of the *ḥajj* season.

Zakāt: A form of religious taxation which has multiples forms including the *zakāt al-fiṭr* which is levied at the completion of the fasting in the Month of *Ramaḍhān*, and other forms mentioned in the books of Islamic jurisprudence.

Ziyārat: Lit. visitation and it refers to the visitation of the shrines and burial sites of the noble men and women such as Prophet Muḥammad, his noble family members, their respected companions and other saintly individuals.

Prophets

English Equivalent	Arabic Name
Aaron	Hārūn
Abraham	Ibrāhīm
Adam	Ādam
David	Dāwūd
Jacob	Yaʿqūb
Jesus	ʿIsā
Jethro	Shuayb
Jonah	Yūnus
Joseph	Yūsuf
Moses	Mūsā
Soloman	Sulaymān

Index

Other Books by the Author

Discovering Islam

A FRESH APPROACH to introducing Islam to the non-Muslim reader, this book introduces Islam by elaborating on the basic tenets of a faith which is practiced by over 1/6 of the world today. The author looks at the 'Pillars of Islam' – the theological beliefs upon which the faith is founded on and then delves into the 'Roots of Islam' – the practices which the believers perform such as prayers, fasting, and almsgiving. The author also goes into an explanation of the various texts of Islam which the Muslims refer to for religious and spiritual guidance. This work ends with providing responses to contemporary questions asked by non-believers concerning social life in Islam, human rights, women's rights, political activism and other important topics.

Monotheism: The Identity of God

MONOTHEISM IS DEFINED as the knowledge of God through the discovery of God's Identity and Attributes. Monotheism is the first step to understanding religion, as without understanding it, the intricate details of religion would be incomprehensible. Recognizing God is the key to understanding His messengers, apostles, scriptures, Divine Justice, the Day of Judgment, and ultimately, our journey and responsibilities in this life. This book is a brief, yet essential, introduction to understanding the theme of monotheism and its branches from an Islamic perspective. Using the Qur'an – God's revealed words – as a major source of discovering God, this book probes many pressing questions, such as: Why does a Merciful and Wise God allow suffering to take place on Earth? Why does such a God allow poverty, pandemics, oppression, and injustice to take over? If God is truly – as monotheists suggest – Omnipotent, Omnipresent, and Omniscient, then why do we not see any intervention from Him to stop crimes, corruption, and different types of miseries all over the world? How can human beings connect with God, and live a fulfilling life of faith in God and service to Him?

Shia Islam

THIS WORK ATTEMPTS to bridge the gap between the Islamic schools of thought by clarifying common misconceptions about Shia Islam, and explaining philosophies and practices specific to the Shia school of thought. These issues are discussed primarily in the light of the Holy Quran and the traditions of the Holy Prophet as related in the books of hadith. The prime goal of this book is to encourage true Muslim unity through dialogue to understand the different ideologies present in Islam today.

From Resolution to Revolution

A COLLECTION OF discussions focusing on the problems and challenges of the current era and solutions to counter them, this work is not just a transcript of 30 lectures delivered in the lunar month of Muharram; rather, it is also a thorough look at the human struggles and experiences which Muslims and non-Muslims face on a day to day basis. Although the words spoken are directed towards a youth audience, other readers will also benefit from this book by understanding the youth of our time. Their unique experiences and challenges in life require an equally unique approach to first define and then solve the social and religious issues that pertain exclusively to them.

When Power and Piety Collide

OVER FOURTEEN HUNDRED years have passed since Prophet Muhammad bonded rival tribes, united neighbors, and partnered the believers to form one community - the Muslim *ummah.* However, since the moment that the final Messenger publicly declared his prophethood and message, the internal relationship of the Muslim *ummah* has yet to fully synthesize. Why is this so? In addition, how can a person better understand the fabric and tendencies of the Muslims? To understand the situation of the Muslims today, an objective and deep look into Islam's history and its key figures is critical. When Power and Piety Collide chronicles the early history of Islam, its development during the life of and shortly after the death of Prophet Muhammad, and then draws an illuminating light on the reasons why Muslims today have yet to establish a fully harmonious *ummah.*

Women - A New Perspective

A DIALOGUE THAT discusses and expounds upon the various issues regarding the rights and laws that pertain to women in Islam, and unwraps some of the distorted images and misconceptions that surround Muslim women. This work has been co-authored with Fatma Saleh, with the various topics presented as a discussion.

Printed in Great Britain
by Amazon

84220391R00100